The **Birchwood Cafe** Cookbook

The **Birchwood Cafe** Cookbook

Tracy Singleton and **Marshall Paulsen**

WITH BETH DOOLEY

PHOTOS BY METTE NIELSEN

University of Minnesota Press
Minneapolis · London

To Lily and Liesl, our toughest critics and most adoring fans
—Tracy and Marshall

Published by the University of Minnesota Press
111 Third Avenue South, Suite 290
Minneapolis, MN 55401-2520
http://www.upress.umn.edu

Library of Congress Cataloging-in-Publication Data
Singleton, Tracy, author.
The Birchwood Cafe cookbook : good real food / Tracy Singleton and Marshall Paulsen ; With Beth Dooley ; Photographs by Mette Nielsen.
Includes bibliographical references and index.
ISBN 978-0-8166-7986-7 (pb)
1. Cooking, American—Midwestern style. 2. Birchwood Cafe (Minneapolis, Minn.) I. Paulsen, Marshall, author. II. Title.
TX715.2.M53S56 2015
641.5977—dc23   2015019108

Book design by bedesign, inc.
Printed in Canada on acid-free paper

The University of Minnesota is an equal-opportunity educator and employer.

22 21 20 19 18 17 16 15

10 9 8 7 6 5 4 3 2 1

CONTENTS

Spring

Summer

GF = gluten free

(V) = vegan

Scorch

Autumn

Dusk

Frost

GF = gluten free

(V) = vegan

Winter

Thaw

The Birchwood Pantry

GF = gluten free

(V) = vegan

"Innumerable measures bring us this [...]
we should know how it comes to us"

— zen meal prayer

GOOD
REAL
FOOD

An Invitation to Cook
from Birchwood Cafe Owner Tracy Singleton

"Innumerable measures bring us this food, we should know how it comes to us."

This Zen meal prayer greets guests as they enter the Birchwood Cafe. It reminds us to be grateful for every farmer, every distributor, everyone who provides us with our ingredients, to honor these relationships and share them with our staff and guests. It reminds us that we are connected to the land, the animals, the environment, and ultimately to each other. Birchwood is more than a restaurant: it is a community, a place where memories are made, ideas are grown, and friends and family connect over Good Real Food.

GOOD REAL FOOD

The Birchwood's mission to serve Good Real Food is also my own. The truth is that I didn't grow up on a farm eating fresh, local, organic food. Back in the mid-1970s and early 1980s, my busy working parents thought low-fat and no-fat packaged ingredients and "boil in the bag" meals were time-saving miracles; I am sure they believed they were good for us too. We spread "I Can't Believe It's Not Butter" on our Wonder Bread and microwaved frozen dinners on hectic school nights.

Summers were different. My fondest childhood memories are of the warmer months spent with my great-grandmother in a small town in Georgia. She was a patient, resourceful cook with a huge garden and orchard. We picked blackberries for cobbler and rolled biscuits by hand. She let me eat that golden farm butter straight from the cut-glass dish. I loved my great-grandmother's food and was always sad to leave her and the warmth and goodness in her kitchen.

Years later, like so many college freshmen in the 1980s, I lived off Diet Mountain Dew and SnackWell's when cramming for exams, and I was completely unaware of and disconnected from my food. When I took a job waiting tables at Lucia's Restaurant in Minneapolis, I began to understand the value of real food and its impact on my own life as well as on the lives of the people who work to grow, cook, serve, and enjoy it.

Lucia Watson is a local food pioneer, and working at her restaurant literally transformed me. I clearly remember my first day on the job. I answered a knock on the back door to see a woman holding plastic garbage bags in each hand, ready to march into the kitchen. I pointed to the dumpster and said, "You know, the trash is over there." She laughed graciously and replied, "No, I'm Kim. I grow the greens." Meeting Kim and all

the purveyors and witnessing talented chefs and bakers at the top of their craft was a revelation. Though I had worked in restaurants since I was fourteen, Lucia's was the first restaurant where I experienced food that came from farmers not factories, food grown with care for the planet, food that truly tasted good. At Lucia's I reconnected to real butter from real cows and revived the long forgotten memories of the made-from-scratch food my great-grandmother fed me many years ago.

I learned a great deal at Lucia's. After hours, my coworkers and I shared dreams of opening a place of our own. When the old Birchwood Grocery in the Seward neighborhood of Minneapolis became available, we jumped on the opportunity to create a cafe that focused on local ingredients and local community—something the original owners had done well for decades. Established as a dairy in 1926 by the Bursch family, the Birchwood employed neighborhood residents and provided milk, butter, and cream to a wider area. As the dairy industry consolidated in the 1940s, the family decided to convert the operation into a neighborhood grocery. It quickly became essential to the neighborhood's life, selling staples, penny candy, and newspapers. Neighbors gathered to catch up with each other, and kids hung out after school. When Cy and Del handed over the keys, we were committed to retaining its generous, welcoming community spirit.

Over the past twenty years, the Birchwood has grown into a community of shared values. We sponsor a bike team, host screenings of films about food issues, ignite crop mobs to help in our farmers' fields, host "know your farmer" events, and work with the Minneapolis Public Schools' True Food Chef Council to provide fresh, healthy, local food in our public school cafeterias. We advocate for

Chef Marshall Paulsen

Birchwood diners savor Minnesota's distinct seasons with Chef Marshall Paulsen's menu. You know that it's Scorch when Sweet Corn Risotto, Cucumber Gazpacho, and the Heirloom Tomato Plate are featured. Come Frost, pumpkins are coated with an icy sheen—time for Pumpkin Hand Pie. When Winter's winds blow, count on Maple Oatmeal Crème Brûlée to help you face the bitter cold day. "You won't find anything with fresh tomatoes in Thaw, nor Brussels sprouts in Spring," Marshall says. "We enjoy so much of our produce when it's in season and available locally. Anything we can't preserve, we anxiously await its return next season."

Marshall's vibrant, accessible cooking shines with the vision of what scratch cooking with local ingredients can be. We collected his recipes here along with his insights and techniques for those savory waffles, tangy sauces, and harmonious vegetable and brown rice combinations. What can you do with tofu? Open these pages and see.

Marshall began his cooking career as a busboy in a country club kitchen in his hometown of St. Paul, Minnesota. He earned his degree in hospitality management from the University of Wisconsin–Stout in Menomonie, Wisconsin. His real education began in a small restaurant outside that college town. "The Creamery Restaurant was surrounded by farms. We got chickens from down the street, trout from up the road, and stopped by the Menomonie Farmer's Market on Saturdays before writing that evening's menu. That's where I met Maurice and Gail of DragSmith Farms, where I first tried Dawn Wood's maple syrup, and learned that foraging in the woods for mushrooms was a thing that people did. The

idea of having everything shipped from a warehouse on a semi would never even occur to us."

Marshall's lucky break came the morning he arrived at the Birchwood to stage (a working interview) for the open sous chef position. I told him the head chef had just been let go and was at my most frazzled when he asked, "Does that mean the chef's job is open?" Long story short, he ended up staying at the restaurant fifteen hours that day, came back the next day, and the next! Lucky for us he has been coming back for nearly a decade.

As Marshall works to shape our menu, the Birchwood also shapes him. He has greatly improved his diet and changed his lifestyle. His patient and respectful approach has helped to make our cafe one of the most desirable places in town to work, where employees and purveyors are trusted collaborators in the day-to-day operation. "We encourage our servers and cooks to partner in creating Good Real Food, as well as to be good people, healthy people, fully present and connected people," he says. "And not just physically, but mentally, spiritually, and emotionally as well."

the labeling of genetically modified foods and for the protection of pollinators, and we help raise funds for organizations that address HIV/AIDS, food justice, and climate change. Our cafe is a CSA drop-off site for eight farms. We work to make our operation environmentally sustainable by composting and recycling more than 90 percent of the cafe's waste and by using both wind and solar energy for our power.

By 2006 we were facing a real problem: the cafe was bursting at the seams. Our kitchen stretched into an offsite location, and we had no storage. Our weekend brunch lines snaked out the door, and the line for our single bathroom wasn't much shorter. It was clear that this business, built on sustainability, was no longer sustainable. We had to grow.

We decided to grow not just bigger but to grow better with energy efficiency, improved working conditions for staff, and more space for groups to gather. We wanted to support more local farmers and serve more Good Real Food, while retaining our intimate, neighborhood vibe. It was a long process to create plans, work with the neighborhood, and secure the necessary permits and zoning.

In 2013 we launched a Kickstarter campaign to bridge the gap in our budget, which was funded from more traditional sources. In thirty short days, we exceeded our goal and became the third-highest-grossing restaurant Kickstarter campaign in the world. Not one to boast, I share this because I am so humbled by the outpouring of love and support that flooded into the Birchwood. We received songs, poems, and stories about the special role the cafe has played in people's lives. Oh, the stories! One customer credits our food for his cancer recovery; others told us of friends and lovers they met in line at the deli counter, of first dates that led to marriage and kids, of celebrating birthdays, anniversaries, and reunions, and of gathering at the restaurant to plan trips around the world.

But none of this would be possible without the food. The food is what connects us to the things that matter and to each other. Our Good Real Food mission is realized each and every day of the week by our talented kitchen staff, led by our executive chef, Marshall Paulsen. He is meticulous and mindful in sourcing ingredients, he makes time to visit our farms, and he knows our purveyors and considers them all his friends. He cooks and he guides our staff with the utmost integrity. Because of Marshall, our menu is innovative yet accessible, elegant yet approachable.

This cookbook is our invitation to bring Birchwood home, to share it with your friends and family, to continue to weave our values into your daily life. All of these recipes are scaled to a home cook, so we intentionally eliminated some of Marshall's steps as well as ingredients that are especially hard to find. We hope the pages get spattered and stuck, dog-eared and marked up. We hope you make new farmer friends as you shop for ingredients. And remember, these recipes are merely guidelines. We are always changing and adapting our menu depending on what comes in from the fields, and we encourage you to do the same. Really, this is nothing new—it's just returning to the way we all used to eat, and it's more important now than ever.

Here's to good real food at home, and here's to you!

With love and gratitude,

Tracy

EATING WITH THE FULLEST pleasure IS PERHAPS THE Profoundest ENACTMENT of OUR connection WITH THE WORLD. —Wendell Berry

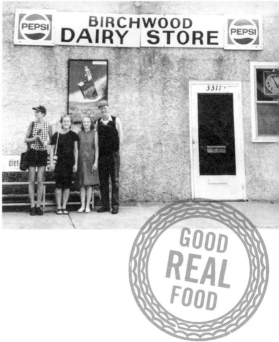

GOOD REAL FOOD

What Is Good Real Food?

At the Birchwood, we create fresh, unique food with down-home appeal. We source local, sustainable, organic, and fair trade ingredients to lovingly handcraft a variety of vegan, vegetarian, and non-vegetarian dishes. We take care to know that the land, the animals, and the people we work with are treated with respect. And we call it "Good Real Food."

GOOD REAL FOOD IS:

- prepared with produce grown locally and sustainably and from animals that had natural, healthy, happy lives
- sourced from farmers, gardeners, and producers with pure hearts and clear intentions
- made from scratch with minimally processed and freshly farmed or foraged ingredients
- created with respect for the integrity and identity of the ingredients, with precise execution and technique, beautiful presentation, and the best flavors possible
- made by the hands of those who have generous souls and the impulse to take care of people
- paired with thought and consideration of what it is being consumed with, where and when it is being consumed, and who is consuming it
- served in a place that supports local agriculture and fair trade practices and offers a place for the community to actively participate in the process of creating and sustaining good food
- eaten by those who care about where their food comes from and how their food is grown, treated, handled, and prepared

We invite you to cook like we do. Get to know your ingredients and where they come from, and bring a little Birchwood home!

A NOTE ABOUT OUR INGREDIENTS

We use locally sourced, sustainably raised ingredients in all of our recipes. We also use seasonal produce from other parts of the world, like citrus fruits, nuts, and grains, and we opt for organic every time. For this reason, we do not call out organic with any of the ingredients, as that is our standard for grains, flours, nut butters, oils, eggs, and dairy.

While our poultry, meat, and fish are not all certified organic, they are always sourced according to our guidelines for Good Real Food. Our beef, pork, and poultry are from small family-run farms that use humane and sustainable practices. Our fish is all sourced using Monterey Bay Aquarium Seafood Watch.

We did not include recipes for stocks, though we rely on our housemade stocks for all of our soups, stews, and sauces. Our stocks vary greatly throughout the season, so it's impossible to provide a standard recipe, and there are plenty of great packaged organic alternatives available on the co-op shelves and from high-quality butcher shops.

We specify rice bran oil in recipes calling for a vegetable oil and extra-virgin olive oil where we want to impart its flavor to the dish. Rice bran oil is a neutral oil that is wonderful for baking and has a high smoke point that makes it perfect for sautéing and stir-frying over high heat. Unlike most other vegetable oils, it does not contain GMOs.

We are working hard to have GMOs labeled, in this state and across the country, and we make every attempt possible to protect our community from exposure to genetically engineered ingredients.

TWIN PONDS · HOCH ORCHARD
WHOLE GRAIN MILLING COMPANY
RIVERBEND FARM · WOODS MAPLE
NATIVE HARVEST · WILD RICE
LAUGHING LOON FARM · MN PEACH
GARDEN FARME ♥ RIVERBEND FARM
FEATHERSTONE FARM · HEARTBEET FARM
STAR PRAIRIE TROUT FARM ♥ EARTHEN PATH ORGANIC FARM ♥
PETERSON LIMOUSIN BEEF · CHERRY TREE HOUSE MUSHROOMS
BULLFROG FISH FARM ♥ CRYSTAL BALL FARMS ORGANIC ♥
COASTAL SEAFOODS · BLUE FRUIT FARM · FERNDALE MARKET ·

LOCAL FARMERS

Using This Cookbook

These recipes reflect the spirit of Birchwood's kitchen but are not written to be exact copies of specific meals. Our menu changes throughout the year, and Marshall is always creating new, innovative dishes. Because there are such tremendous differences in fresh foods, we all work with a range of variables. The blueberries we used to test a recipe may differ in size and sweetness from those you picked yourself on the North Shore. Add to this variations in the temperatures of different ovens, pot sizes, and so on—nothing is precise or predictable.

We attempted to make these recipes as user-friendly as possible, so we were careful to keep them simple, avoiding lengthy steps and hard-to-find ingredients. Birchwood Cafe's food is unique, impossible to replicate in a home kitchen. We hope this book will inspire you to cook, Birchwood style. The recipes are guidelines, so taste, adjust, and make them your own!

GOOD REAL FOOD

GOOD REAL FOOD

SPRING

Spring is the season for hopeful cooks: full of possibility, earth's promise is fulfilled. After the long, frozen winter, the root cellar now depleted, the pantry shelves picked bare, here come the delicate greens, the fiddleheads and rhubarb, poking tentatively up through the cold earth. But these plants are resilient, and so are we. Bring on the asparagus, the fresh eggs from hens once again laying, the ramps so strong their fragrance announces their presence. Let's hunt morels in the damp woods to sauté over an open fire in lots of golden butter; we'll scoop them out of the iron skillet with a hunk of hearty wheat bread. Pretty soon we'll have snow peas, spring onions, garlic scapes, a lush carpet of lettuces, radishes with peppery crunch, basil and parsley, thyme and marjoram. As the sun grows stronger, we do too, reclaiming our vigor and strength.

Asparagus, Cheddar, and Quinoa Savory Waffle

GF Serves 6 to 8

Light, crunchy, and full of character, this waffle is wonderful even if you're not concerned with wheat. It's gluten free but full of flavor, shot through with roasted asparagus and laced with cheddar cheese. It's perfect for brunch or a lovely light supper.

½ cup quinoa

1 cup brown rice flour

1 cup quinoa flour

½ cup potato starch

¼ cup arrowroot starch flour

1 tablespoon xanthan gum

1 teaspoon salt

1 tablespoon baking powder

6 tablespoons rice bran oil, plus extra for the waffle iron

3 cups buttermilk, or more if needed

3 large eggs, lightly beaten

½ cup shredded cheddar cheese

⅓ pound (about 8 to 10 spears) asparagus, chopped and roasted (see note)

In a small skillet set over medium heat, toast ¼ cup of the quinoa, shaking the pan occasionally, until it is light brown, about 1 to 2 minutes. Steep the other ¼ cup of quinoa in boiling water for 5 minutes, and then drain it.

In a large bowl, stir together the rice flour, quinoa flour, potato starch, arrowroot, xanthan gum, toasted quinoa, salt, and baking powder.

In a separate bowl, whisk together the oil, buttermilk, and eggs. Pour the wet ingredients into the flour mixture, and stir until smooth. The batter will be thick. Stir in the steeped quinoa, cheese, and asparagus.

Preheat the oven to 200 degrees. Heat up the waffle iron and lightly brush the cooking surfaces with oil. When the waffle iron is ready, pour in 1 cup of batter. Cook until the waffle is lightly browned, about 5 to 6 minutes. Transfer the waffle to a baking sheet and keep it warm, uncovered, in the oven until ready to serve. Repeat with the remaining batter.

Serve the waffles with a dollop of Lemon Pepita Butter (page 88) and Rhubarb Jalapeño Marmalade (page 216).

COOK'S NOTE

TO ROAST ASPARAGUS: Preheat the oven to 375 degrees. Cut the asparagus into quarter-inch pieces, and toss it with just enough rice bran oil to coat. Spread out the asparagus on a baking sheet, and roast until it is nicely browned and crisp around the edges, about 5 to 10 minutes.

Spring Egg Scramble GF Serves 4

Oh, the possibilities for scrambles are endless, all year long! Here's our basic scramble recipe, bright with chopped fennel and radishes, plus lots of dill. Vary the veggies to use whatever you have on hand. Serve with fresh spring greens tossed with Green Tea Vinaigrette.

8 large eggs

1 tablespoon fresh minced dill

Salt and freshly ground black pepper

1 tablespoon unsalted butter

1 small fennel bulb, diced

3 to 4 French radishes, sliced
(¼ cup)

½ cup shelled fresh peas, or frozen
peas, thawed

¼ cup crumbled feta

2 to 3 ounces watercress (2 cups)

2 to 3 ounces arugula (2 cups)

¼ cup Green Tea Vinaigrette
(page 234)

In a medium bowl, whisk together the eggs, dill, and salt and pepper.

Heat the butter in a 10-inch skillet set over moderate heat. Add the fennel and cook until softened, about 2 to 3 minutes. Stir in the radishes and peas, and sauté a minute or two. Add the eggs and cook, stirring, until just heated through, about 4 to 6 minutes. Stir in the feta.

In a medium bowl, toss the watercress and arugula with just enough Green Tea Vinaigrette to lightly coat the greens. Serve the greens alongside the scramble.

Smoked Trout Quiche Serves 6 to 8

At the Birchwood, we smoke our own trout, but you'll find wonderful smoked trout in local natural food co-ops and from fish shops along the North Shore—and, of course, from Bullfrog Fish Farm (see page 6). Pair this quiche with a salad of fresh peppery watercress, one of the first greens available at farmers markets.

1 Basic Pastry Crust (recipe follows)
1 tablespoon rice bran oil
1 large or 2 small shallots, chopped (½ cup)
1 cup flaked smoked trout
4 large eggs
2 large egg yolks

3 cups half-and-half
2 tablespoons chopped parsley
1 tablespoon chopped fresh thyme
2 teaspoons grated lemon zest
Pinch of red pepper flakes
Pinch of salt

Preheat the oven to 400 degrees. On a lightly floured surface, roll out the crust about ¼ inch thick and fit it into a deep 9-inch quiche or pie tin, folding the edge under to leave about ¼ inch above the rim. Prick the pastry all over with a fork. Line the pastry with foil or parchment paper, and then cover it with pie weights or dried beans or rice. Bake until lightly golden, about 20 minutes. Remove the foil and weights, and return the pastry to the oven to bake an additional 10 minutes. Let it cool on a rack.

Heat the oil in a small skillet set over medium heat, and sauté the shallots until they are lightly browned, about 5 minutes.

Sprinkle the shallots over the crust; then arrange the fish over the shallots. In a medium bowl, whisk together the eggs, egg yolks, half-and-half, parsley, thyme, lemon zest, red pepper, and salt. Pour the egg mixture over the trout and shallots. Bake until a knife inserted in the center comes out clean, about 50 minutes. Allow to cool 10 minutes before serving.

Basic Pastry Crust

Makes a single 9- to 10-inch crust

We use this crust for our quiches and pies. The dough is easy to work with and will keep several days in the refrigerator wrapped tightly in parchment paper or plastic wrap.

1 ⅓ cups unbleached all-purpose flour

¼ teaspoon salt

¼ teaspoon sugar

½ cup (1 stick) cold unsalted butter, cut into pieces

3 ounces cold cream cheese, cut into pieces

2 to 3 tablespoons ice water

In a medium bowl, whisk together the flour, salt, and sugar. Cut the butter and cream cheese into the flour mixture to make coarse crumbs. Stir in just enough ice water to bring the mixture together. Gather the dough into a ball, wrap it in parchment paper, and chill it in the refrigerator for at least 20 minutes before rolling it out.

Bullfrog Fish Farm
Menomonie, Wisconsin

Bullfrog Fish Farm catches the best acts in town on its calendar of "hoots and happenings," which attract crowds to its shore lunches with live music and a beer garden, all centered near its ponds. Visitors can catch their own trout or let the crew catch, clean, and pack them for carryout. **Herby Radmann** decided a long time ago that the best way to educate is to entertain.

The farm produces twenty thousand pounds of fresh fish per year, selling both fresh and smoked fish to the community and surrounding restaurants. With his "Eat My Fish" attitude, Herby has come to understand and communicate the challenges of small rural businesses and inspires pride in the Chippewa Valley.

Bullfrog
FISH FARM
Smokin' GOOD
RAINBOW TROUT

Carrot Ginger Soup (V) GF Serves 6 to 8

We can't keep this soup in stock: as soon as we fill the deli case with containers to go, we run out. Fortunately, this recipe is easy to multiply to feed a crowd. This soup is creamy but contains no cream.

2 tablespoons rice bran oil
3 inches ginger, grated
    (3 tablespoons)
3 cloves garlic, minced
2 pounds carrots, cut into 1-inch
    pieces
1 tablespoon coriander
5 ½ cups vegetable stock

1 cup coconut milk
½ cup fresh orange juice
1 tablespoon grated orange zest
1 to 2 teaspoons brown sugar
Salt and freshly ground black pepper
Pinch of red pepper flakes
Chopped cilantro for garnish

Heat the oil in a large soup pot set over medium-high heat, and sauté the ginger, garlic, and carrots until they begin to soften, about 2 minutes. Stir in the coriander and the stock. Bring the stock to a simmer, and cook until the carrots are soft, about 15 minutes.

Working in small batches, puree the soup in a blender and return it to the pot. Stir in the coconut milk, orange juice, orange zest, and brown sugar, adding more stock if necessary. Season to taste with salt, pepper, and red pepper flakes. Serve garnished with chopped cilantro.

COOK'S NOTE

HOT SOUP SEEMS TO EXPLODE IN THE BLENDER! Always work in small batches when blending hot liquids.

Potato Beet Salad (V) GF Serves 4 to 6

This salad is as pretty as it is easy to make. It's wonderful for a spring dinner and can be served warm, at room temperature, or chilled.

¼ cup apple cider vinegar

1 tablespoon whole-grain Dijon mustard

2 teaspoons honey

½ cup rice bran oil

1 large carrot, sliced diagonally

½ cup shelled fresh peas, or frozen peas, thawed

1 pound red or Yukon Gold potatoes

1 pound golden beets

½ cup chopped red onion

2 tablespoons chopped fresh dill

Salt and freshly ground black pepper

In a small bowl, whisk together the cider, mustard, and honey; then whisk in the oil. Set the vinaigrette aside.

Place the carrots in a small pot, and add water to cover. Bring the water to a boil, and cook until the carrots are bright and just tender, about 2 to 3 minutes. Drain and set aside.

In a small pot, bring some water to a boil. Blanch the peas about 1 minute for fresh peas, 30 seconds for frozen. Drain and set aside.

Cook the potatoes and beets in separate saucepans of boiling water until just tender, about 30 minutes for the potatoes and 45 minutes for the beets. Drain and let cool slightly before peeling and cutting into ½-inch cubes. Turn the cooked vegetables into a big bowl along with the red onion and dill, and toss with just enough vinaigrette to coat. Season with salt and pepper.

Pesto Perfect! Makes 1 to 1 ½ cups

Keep these pestos on hand for tossing into pasta, topping burgers,
swirling into mayonnaise for sandwiches, and blending into yogurt
for dips. They keep beautifully in the refrigerator and make everyday
meals a little brighter. Make pesto as fresh herbs come into the garden
throughout the season. Did we say that these pestos freeze nicely too?

Sun-Dried Tomato Pesto GF

1 cup sun-dried tomatoes

2 cloves minced garlic

2 tablespoons grated Parmesan
  cheese

1 teaspoon lemon juice

2 tablespoons extra-virgin olive oil,
  or more as needed

Salt and freshly ground black pepper

Soak the tomatoes in 2 cups of warm water until they have softened,
about 15 to 20 minutes. Drain the tomatoes.

Put all of the ingredients into a food processor fitted with a steel blade
and puree, adding more oil if necessary.

Arugula Basil Pesto GF

3 large cloves garlic

½ cup pine nuts

½ cup coarsely grated Parmesan
  cheese

2 cups basil leaves

1 cup arugula leaves

⅔ cup extra-virgin olive oil

Salt and freshly ground black pepper

Chop the garlic cloves in a food processor fitted with a steel blade; then
add the pine nuts, cheese, basil, and arugula and process until finely
chopped. Pulse in the oil until it is incorporated but the pesto is not
completely smooth. Season to taste with salt and black pepper.

Cilantro Cashew Pesto (V) GF

2 ½ cups cilantro leaves

2 cloves garlic

½ cup raw cashews

2 tablespoons lime juice

½ cup rice bran oil

Salt and freshly ground black pepper

Put the cilantro, garlic, cashews, and lime juice into a food processor
fitted with a steel blade. Process, slowly adding the oil to reach the
desired consistency. Season to taste with salt and black pepper.

Mint Jalapeño Pesto GF

½ cup whole raw almonds

1 cup mint leaves

2 cloves garlic

1 small jalapeño, seeded, veined, and chopped

½ cup grated Parmesan cheese

2 tablespoons fresh orange juice

½ cup rice bran oil

Salt and freshly ground black pepper

Preheat the oven to 350 degrees. Spread the almonds on a baking sheet, and toast them until they are slightly browned, about 10 minutes.

Put the almonds, mint, garlic, jalapeño, cheese, and orange juice into a food processor fitted with a steel blade. Process until the almonds are coarsely ground. Slowly add the oil in a steady stream, processing until roughly combined. Season to taste with salt and black pepper.

Watercress Mint Chermoula (Moroccan Pesto) (V) GF

1 cup watercress

½ cup mint leaves

¼ cup Preserved Lemons (page 228)

1 teaspoon cumin

1 teaspoon coriander

1 teaspoon caraway

1 teaspoon paprika

½ cup extra-virgin olive oil

Salt and freshly ground black pepper

Put the watercress, mint, lemon, cumin, coriander, caraway, and paprika in a food processor fitted with a steel blade. Process to chop the leaves, and then add the oil in a slow stream. Season to taste with salt and pepper. The chermoula will keep about a day or two in the refrigerator.

PESTO IN ACTION

PASTA: Put ⅔ cup of pesto in a large bowl with 1 pound of cooked, hot pasta and a little of the pasta cooking water. Toss and serve with grated cheese.

MAYONNAISE: Swirl 2 to 3 tablespoons of pesto into 1 cup of mayonnaise to use on sandwiches and wraps.

DIPS: Swirl 2 to 3 tablespoons of pesto into ½ cup of sour cream or yogurt plus ¼ cup of mayonnaise. Our friend and farmer Mary Reynolds shared this tip for freezing pesto. Line a baking sheet with parchment paper. Spread the pesto over the paper, and freeze until hard. Cut the pesto into squares or break it into pieces to store in freezer bags.

Spring Vegetable Pizza Serves 4 to 6

This lovely, light pizza featuring our White Bean Spread is a great starter or light meal. The marinated beans taste best when made a day or two ahead; double the batch so you have some to use in salads. White Bean Spread is also an excellent dip for vegetables and chips.

Marinated White Beans

¼ cup cider vinegar

¼ cup minced parsley

¼ cup extra-virgin olive oil

1 cup cooked navy beans

2 cloves garlic, minced

1 small shallot, minced

¼ cup drained and minced Pickled
   Peppers (page 225)

Salt and freshly ground black pepper

White Bean Spread

1 cup cooked navy beans

2 cloves garlic, minced

1 teaspoon cumin

1 teaspoon cider vinegar

½ cup reserved bean water or
   vegetable stock

1 to 2 tablespoons heavy cream

Salt and freshly ground black pepper

Pizza

Cornmeal

Birchwood Pizza and Flatbread
   Dough (page 147)

½ pound hakurei turnips with their
   greens, cut into half-inch pieces
   and blanched

½ pound asparagus cut into half-
   inch pieces and blanched

½ cup shredded cheddar cheese

Roasted Meyer Lemon Oil (page 230)

Green Tea Vinaigrette (page 234)

continued on page 16

continued from page 14

Make the Marinated White Beans. Whisk together the vinegar, parsley, and oil. Toss in the beans and the remaining ingredients. Season to taste with salt and freshly ground black pepper. Let stand at room temperature for at least an hour, or cover and refrigerate for several days so the seasonings marry.

Make the White Bean Spread. In a food processor fitted with a steel blade, process the beans, garlic, cumin, and vinegar with a little of the reserved bean water. Add a little heavy cream to enrich the spread. Season with salt and freshly ground black pepper.

Preheat the oven to 425 degrees. Dust a pizza peel or a rimless baking sheet with cornmeal. On a lightly floured surface, roll out the dough into a 9- to 10-inch circle, and then place it on the pizza peel. Gently shake the peel back and forth to make sure the crust is not sticking; then transfer the crust to the oven rack. Bake the crust until it is firm and crusty brown, about 10 to 15 minutes.

Spread the crust with White Bean Spread. Spoon the Marinated White Beans on top. Arrange the blanched turnips and asparagus over the beans. Scatter the cheese over the vegetables. Return the pizza to the oven to melt the cheese, about 5 minutes. Remove the pizza from the oven, and drizzle it with Roasted Meyer Lemon Oil and Green Tea Vinaigrette. Serve hot.

TO BLANCH VEGETABLES, plunge them in a pot of rapidly boiling water just until the color brightens. Asparagus and turnips will need about 30 seconds to 1 minute. Drain, and shock the vegetables in ice-cold water.

Turkey Salad with Avocado Puree GF Serves 4

This simple salad, with its vibrant green, lime-kissed avocado puree and plenty of cilantro, takes the turkey sandwich to another level. Serve the turkey salad on whole wheat bread or focaccia spread with the avocado puree. Or serve the salad on a bed of dark greens garnished with the avocado puree—this makes a bright addition to a luncheon buffet.

Turkey Salad

7 to 8 ounces cooked turkey, diced (1 ½ cups)

1 stalk celery, diced

¼ cup diced red onion

½ cup mayonnaise

¼ cup chopped cilantro

1 tablespoon lime juice plus a little extra for seasoning

¼ cup toasted pepitas, lightly ground

Salt and freshly ground black pepper

Avocado Puree

2 avocados

2 tablespoons lime juice

Salt and freshly ground black pepper

In a large bowl, toss together the turkey, celery, and onion. Stir in the mayonnaise, cilantro, lime juice, and ground pepitas. Season to taste with salt, pepper, and more lime juice.

Halve the avocados, remove the pits, and scoop the fruit into a food processor fitted with a steel blade. Process in the lime juice, and then season with salt and pepper.

DragSmith Farms
Barron, Wisconsin

I f anyone can grow artichokes in this part of the country, **Gail and Maurice Smith** are the ones to do so. DragSmith Farms provides the Twin Cities metro area with a vast array of microgreens and lettuces grown throughout the year in its vast hoop houses. No matter how hard March winds blow, DragSmith keeps us all in the green—pea greens, baby mizuna, kale, mustard, arugula. The Smiths also deliver local food from nearby farms to co-ops and restaurants. Thanks to them, we can all share great eggs, trout, dairy, and bison throughout the year.

Millet-Crusted Trout GF Serves 4

This dish is a favorite of Ali Selim, writer, director, and producer of the movie *Sweet Land*. He is a member of the Birchwood Bike Team and credits Birchwood's healthy, active lifestyle for helping him recover from cancer. "Birchwood taught me how to eat to thrive," he says.

We're lucky to live near so many organic farms, like Bullfrog Fish Farm in Menomonie, Wisconsin, that raise trout as part of their enclosed ecosystem. We serve this simple dish on a soft bed of Red Pepper Chickpea Puree (page 22), garnished with shaved radishes and fennel.

1 cup millet

2 large eggs

4 small whole trout, cleaned (heads and tails left intact), rinsed, and patted dry

Salt and freshly ground black pepper

2 tablespoons rice bran oil

1 to 2 stalks rhubarb, chopped (½ cup)

3 to 4 ounces salad greens (2 cups)

½ cup Orange Honey Vinaigrette (page 234)

Shaved radish and fennel and chopped almonds for garnish

Spread the millet on a plate. Lightly beat the egg in a pie plate.

Season the trout inside and out with salt and pepper. Dip both sides of each fish first in the egg and then in the millet to coat. Heat the oil in a 12-inch skillet over moderate heat until hot but not smoking. Add the trout and cook, shaking the skillet occasionally to prevent sticking and turning once with a spatula, until browned on both sides and just cooked through, about 12 minutes total.

Put the rhubarb in a small saucepan with just enough water to cover. Bring to a boil and poach until tender, about 2 minutes. Drain, and stir into the Orange Honey Vinaigrette.

Serve the trout on a bed of Red Pepper Chickpea Puree. Garnish the trout with the greens, shaved radish and fennel, chopped almonds, and a drizzle of the poached rhubarb.

Red Pepper Chickpea Puree

GF Serves 4

This is a lush accompaniment to Millet-Crusted Trout (page 21), but it's also delicious as a topping for bruschetta or as a dip for toast.

1 cup cooked chickpeas

1 medium red pepper, roasted and coarsely chopped (½ cup; see note)

¼ cup whole-milk yogurt

2 tablespoons tomato paste

¼ cup extra-virgin olive oil

1 tablespoon ground fennel

Salt and freshly ground black pepper

Chopped cilantro for garnish

Puree the chickpeas, roasted red pepper, yogurt, tomato paste, olive oil, and fennel in a food processor fitted with a steel blade. Season the puree to taste with salt and black pepper. Garnish the puree with cilantro, and serve it alongside the trout or as a dip.

COOK'S NOTE

TO ROAST PEPPERS, SWEET OR HOT, place the peppers directly on a flame (on the grill, under the broiler, or over a gas burner). Turn until the entire pepper is completely charred. Place the pepper in a small brown paper bag or wrap it in a clean kitchen towel and allow it to cool. Remove the charred skin of the pepper, and then split it open and remove the veins and seeds. One large red pepper will yield about ¾ to 1 cup of chopped roasted pepper. These will store for a week in a covered container.

Rhubarb Pecan Bars Makes about 16 bars

These bars are soft and delicious, tangy with the taste of fresh rhubarb. Serve them any time of day. (They are great at breakfast!)

2 cups unbleached all-purpose flour

1 teaspoon baking powder

½ teaspoon baking soda

1 teaspoon cinnamon

½ teaspoon freshly grated nutmeg

½ teaspoon salt

½ cup (1 stick) unsalted butter, at room temperature

1 ¼ cups sugar

1 teaspoon vanilla extract

3 large eggs

1 cup plain Greek-style yogurt

3 to 4 stalks rhubarb, finely chopped (1 cup)

½ cup toasted chopped pecans

Powdered sugar for garnish

Preheat the oven to 325 degrees. Lightly grease a 9-inch-square baking pan, or line it with parchment paper.

In a medium bowl, whisk together the flour, baking powder, baking soda, cinnamon, nutmeg, and salt. In a separate bowl, cream the butter and sugar until it is light and fluffy, and then beat in the vanilla. Beat in the eggs one at a time. Beginning and ending with the flour mixture, alternately fold portions of the flour mixture and the yogurt into the butter mixture. Fold in the rhubarb and the pecans.

Scrape the batter into the prepared baking pan and spread it evenly; then tap the pan on the counter to release any air bubbles. Bake until a wooden toothpick inserted near the center comes up clean, about 50 to 55 minutes. Cool on a wire rack. Dust with sifted powdered sugar before serving.

Rhubarb Brown Sugar Scones

Makes 8 scones

Serve these tender scones with lots of strawberry jam. They are also a fabulous base for strawberry shortcake served with tons of vanilla whipped cream and tiny local berries.

1 ⅔ cups unbleached all-purpose flour

¼ cup brown sugar

2 ½ teaspoons baking powder

¼ teaspoon salt

1 cup heavy cream, plus a little extra for brushing over the dough

1 teaspoon vanilla extract

1 to 2 stalks rhubarb, finely chopped (½ cup)

Rolled oats for garnish

Sugar for garnish

Preheat the oven to 450 degrees. Line a baking sheet with parchment paper. In a large bowl, whisk together the flour, brown sugar, baking powder, and salt. In a small bowl, whisk together the cream and the vanilla.

Make a well in the center of the flour mixture, and pour in the cream and vanilla. Gently stir in the rhubarb. Combine with just a few stirs of a fork. With one hand, press the dough against the sides of the bowl to gather up the flour and bring the dough together.

Turn the dough out onto the parchment paper and gently press the dough into an 8-inch round. Lightly brush the top with the extra cream, and sprinkle it with the oats and sugar. Cut the round into 8 wedges. Bake until golden, about 13 to 15 minutes.

SUMMER

Suddenly it's summer! We're nearly giddy with the heat. Lettuces, peas, and delicate plants give way to strawberries, green beans, and snap peas ripening on the vine, while the kohlrabi, cucumbers, and summer squash come in at a galloping pace. Who has time to cook? Truth is, there's no need to. With produce at its peak, so fresh, so good, all a cook needs to do is step out of the way and let the natural flavors shine. We'll roast those bitty, marble-sized baby potatoes, grill zucchini from the garden, and panfry fish straight from the lake. You'll see the Birchwood Bike Team everywhere, pedaling River Road, the Greenway, all around town, then returning to the cafe in time to watch the Tour de France. Vive le Brunch! Why wait? Get your summer on!

Egg and Bacon Sandwich Serves 8

This hale and hearty sandwich, seasoned with a dollop of Birchwood Aioli, sports a sunny-side up egg on top of applewood smoked bacon. Be sure to use farm-fresh eggs and artisan bacon (cooked super crisp). We serve this on soft buttermilk buns.

1 pound applewood smoked bacon

2 tablespoons unsalted butter

8 farm-fresh eggs

8 buns

½ cup Birchwood Aioli (page 239)

4 ounces microgreens

In a large skillet, cook the bacon over medium heat until it is very crisp, about 10 minutes. Drain the bacon on paper towels.

Remove the bacon grease from the skillet, add the butter, and return the pan to the heat to melt the butter. Working in batches, cook the eggs sunny-side up, about 4 minutes for medium-firm eggs. Vary the cooking time to cook the eggs to your liking.

Slather the buns with the aioli, then pile in the microgreens, bacon, and eggs.

WHY ARE FRESH EGGS SO IMPORTANT TO US? First, because of their true, sunny color and eggy flavor. Next, because of the high level of omega-3 fatty acids. And finally, because we like knowing that the chickens are well cared for, that they can get outside and peck in the grass and act like chickens. We want the animals we depend on to be treated with respect.

Vive la France French Toast with Macerated Berries and Honey-Roasted Almonds Serves 6 to 8

The vibrant blue and red of the berries with fresh white cream is our homage to the flag of France, home of the greatest bike race on earth, the Tour de France.

Use a rich egg bread or brioche for this custardy French toast. Baking it in a dish keeps it from drying out and makes it especially easy to serve. Prepare the French toast and the fruit the night before, and let them rest in the refrigerator. The almonds can be prepared ahead, too.

Macerated Berries

1 pint strawberries, hulled and quartered

1 pint blueberries

2 tablespoons sugar

1 tablespoon lemon juice

2 tablespoons Grand Marnier

2 tablespoons Chambord

French Toast

6 to 8 thick slices brioche or egg bread

5 tablespoons unsalted butter, melted

4 large eggs

2 egg yolks

4 cups half-and-half

¼ cup honey

2 teaspoons vanilla extract

Pinch of grated nutmeg

Vanilla Whipped Cream

1 cup whipping cream

2 tablespoons sugar

1 teaspoon vanilla extract

Honey-Roasted Almonds (page 35)

Make the Macerated Berries. Put all of the ingredients into a medium bowl, cover, and refrigerate about 8 hours, or overnight.

To make the French Toast, brush both sides of the bread slices with butter and place them in a 9 × 13-inch baking dish. In a large bowl, beat the eggs and egg yolks; then whisk in the half-and-half, honey, vanilla, and nutmeg. Pour the egg mixture over the bread. Cover and chill for at least 1 hour, or overnight. Remove from the refrigerator about 30 minutes before baking.

Preheat the oven to 350 degrees. Bake the French Toast, uncovered, until a sharp knife inserted in the center comes up clean, about 35 to 40 minutes. Allow the French Toast to cool about 10 minutes before cutting it into squares to serve.

To make the Vanilla Whipped Cream, put the cream in a bowl, add the sugar and the vanilla, and whip until soft peaks form, about 3 minutes.

To assemble the French Toast, put a square on each plate, and top it with macerated berries, whipped cream, and a sprinkling of almonds.

Chilled Sweet Pea and Mint Soup

(V) GF Serves 4 to 6

This soup is as pretty as it is tasty. Serve it in mugs or bowls garnished with radish slices, fresh mint and pea tendrils, or crushed pistachios.

3 tablespoons rice bran oil

1 medium onion, chopped

4 cups vegetable stock

6 cups shelled fresh peas, or frozen peas, thawed

¼ cup chopped parsley

⅓ cup chopped mint

½ cup coconut milk

Salt and freshly ground black pepper

2 tablespoons lemon juice, or more to taste

2 to 3 small radishes, sliced

Roasted Meyer Lemon Oil (page 230)

In a large, deep, heavy pot, heat the oil over medium-high and sauté the onion until it's soft, about 5 minutes. Stir in the stock and the peas, reduce the heat, and simmer until the peas are tender, about 5 minutes for fresh or 2 minutes for frozen.

Remove the pot from the heat. Add the parsley, mint, and coconut milk. Working in small batches, transfer the soup to a blender and puree it. Return the soup to the pot and season it with salt and pepper and lemon juice. Allow the soup to cool to room temperature, and then chill it until ready to serve. Garnish the soup with radish slices and a drizzle of Roasted Meyer Lemon Oil.

Strawberry Salad with Garlic Chèvre Mousse GF Serves 6

Here's our spin on the strawberry spinach salad. Instead of feta, a distinctive chèvre mousse adds a creamy tang. The mousse also makes a great spread on sandwiches, or try it as a topping on pizza. Honey-Roasted Almonds add a fine touch. To take this salad over the top, fry up some bacon to crumble over it.

Garlic Chèvre Mousse

¼ cup poached garlic (page 194)

4 ounces cream cheese

½ cup chèvre

1 tablespoon heavy cream

Salt and freshly ground black pepper

Salad

5 ounces baby spinach

¼ cup sliced basil leaves

Strawberry White Balsamic Vinaigrette (page 236)

½ pint strawberries, hulled and sliced (1 cup)

Honey-Roasted Almonds (page 35)

To make the Garlic Chèvre Mousse, put the poached garlic, cream cheese, and chèvre into the bowl of a stand mixer and add a splash of heavy cream. Using the whip attachment, beat on high until light and fluffy. Season with salt and pepper to taste, and set aside.

To assemble the salad, put the spinach and basil into a large bowl, and toss with just enough of the vinaigrette to coat the leaves. Toss in the strawberries. Arrange the salad on a large platter or on individual serving plates, and garnish with a scoop of Garlic Chèvre Mousse and Honey-Roasted Almonds.

Honey-Roasted Almonds (V) GF Makes 2 cups

Careful—these are dangerous. Think about doubling the batch, because only about half the nuts we roast actually make it out of the kitchen. These almonds are a terrific finish to the Strawberry Salad with Garlic Chèvre Mousse (page 34).

2 cups whole raw almonds
¼ cup honey
2 tablespoons rice bran oil

2 tablespoons sesame seeds
¼ teaspoon kosher salt

Line a baking sheet with parchment paper, and spread the almonds in a single layer. Place the pan in a cold oven. Turn the oven to 350 degrees and bake, stirring occasionally, until the almonds are light and fragrant, about 12 to 15 minutes. The nuts will continue to cook after removing them from the oven.

Meanwhile, stir together the honey and the oil in a pot large enough to hold the almonds. Set the pot over medium heat, bring the honey to a boil, then reduce the heat to medium-low and simmer for 2 minutes, stirring occasionally. Stir in the almonds, and simmer an additional 2 minutes. Remove from the heat, and spread the almonds on the baking sheet again. Sprinkle the almonds with the sesame seeds and salt, turning to coat. Allow to cool completely.

COOK'S NOTE

FOR HONEY-ROASTED WALNUTS, simply substitute walnuts for almonds in this recipe.

Tour de France Turkey Burger

Serves 4

Thinly sliced Lonza (dry-cured pork) makes this burger the talk of the tour. The Lonza comes from Red Table Meat Co. in Northeast Minneapolis, founded by Mike Phillips (a former Birchwood Bike Team cyclist). Red Table sources whole pigs from small, sustainable farms and collaborates with farmers to honor the pig from farrow and feed to humane slaughter. Then Mike and his crew ply their craft to create the most authentic, best-tasting cured meat around.

We also often top this burger with crisp bacon, an equally winning combination.

Turkey Burgers

1 tablespoon extra-virgin olive oil	1 ⅓ pounds ground turkey
2 cloves garlic, chopped	1 teaspoon ground black pepper
1 large shallot, chopped	1 teaspoon salt
1 stalk celery, leaves included, chopped	Rice bran oil for frying the burgers

Red Grape Rosemary Salsa

4 cups red grapes	1 small bunch green onions, coarsely chopped (¼ cup)
1 tablespoon fresh rosemary leaves	
2 cloves garlic	Salt and freshly ground black pepper

Blue Cheese Walnut Spread

½ cup crumbled blue cheese	¼ cup cream cheese
⅓ cup walnuts, toasted at 350 degrees for 10 minutes	2 tablespoons heavy cream or half-and-half
¼ cup sour cream	Salt and freshly ground black pepper

continued on page 38

continued from page 36

Roasted Scape Mayo

¼ pound garlic scapes

Rice bran oil

½ cup mayonnaise

Salt and freshly ground black pepper

4 of your favorite buns

8 thin slices Lonza or crisp bacon

4 ounces microgreens

Heat the olive oil in a small skillet set over medium heat. Add the garlic, shallot, and celery, and sauté until soft, about 2 minutes.

Put the ground turkey in a medium bowl, and work in the sautéed vegetables and salt and pepper. Portion out 4 burgers and form them into patties. With your thumb, press a dimple into the middle of each patty. Set the patties aside.

For the Red Grape Rosemary Salsa, put the grapes, rosemary, garlic, and green onions into a food processor fitted with a steel blade, and pulse several times to coarsely chop. Season to taste with salt and pepper.

For the Blue Cheese Walnut Spread, put the blue cheese, walnuts, sour cream, cream cheese, and cream into a food processor fitted with a steel blade. Process, adding more cream if needed. Season the spread with salt and pepper, and set it aside.

For the Roasted Scape Mayo, preheat the oven to 350 degrees. In a medium bowl, toss the garlic scapes with a little oil, and then spread them out on a roasting pan. Roast until tender and beginning to brown, about 5 to 8 minutes. Transfer the scapes to a cutting board and mince them. Put the minced scapes in a small bowl, stir in the mayonnaise, and season to taste with salt and pepper.

To cook the burgers, heat a large skillet or griddle and brush it with rice bran oil. Fry the burgers until they are cooked through, about 5 minutes per side. The meat should register 165 degrees on a meat thermometer.

Spread the bottom half of each bun with Blue Cheese Walnut Spread. Set a cooked burger on top of the spread. Then put Red Grape Rosemary Salsa on top of the turkey burger, followed by the Lonza (or bacon) and microgreens. Spread the top half of the bun with Roasted Scape Mayo, and top off the sandwich. Serve immediately. Provide plenty of napkins—this is a two-fisted affair.

Sesame Green Bean and Quinoa Salad (V) GF Serves 4 to 6

Make this salad when green beans are at their peak. The brilliant colors of the fresh vegetables are a striking contrast to the red quinoa. This salad will keep at least a day in the refrigerator.

Salad

1 pound green beans, tipped and tailed

1 ½ cups red quinoa

1 small yellow onion, thinly sliced

½ pound cherry tomatoes, quartered (1 cup)

¼ cup minced green onions

Sesame Tamari Vinaigrette (page 237)

⅓ cup chopped toasted almonds

⅛ cup black sesame seeds

⅛ cup white sesame seeds

To blanch the beans, bring a large pot of heavily salted water to a boil over high heat. Plunge the beans into the boiling water, cooking only until they turn bright green, about 1 to 2 minutes. Drain, and then shock the beans in a bowl of ice-cold water.

Before cooking the quinoa, put the grain in a fine mesh sieve and rinse it under running water for a few minutes. Turn the quinoa into a medium pot, and cover it with 2 inches of water. Set the pot over high heat, and bring the water to a boil. Reduce the heat, cover, and simmer until the quinoa is tender, about 10 to 15 minutes. Drain and set aside.

To assemble the salad, put the green beans and quinoa into a large bowl. Toss in the onion, tomatoes, and green onions, and drizzle in enough vinaigrette to lightly coat the vegetables. Serve garnished with chopped almonds and sesame seeds.

Shepherd's Way Farms
Nerstrand, Minnesota

Arriving at Shepherd's Way Farms is like entering a long-ago era. Chickens flutter near the barn set on the edge of a wide pasture where the sheep graze. Cheese maker **Jodi Ohlsen Read** and her husband, **Steven Read**, raise more than one hundred dairy sheep for the cheeses Jodi crafts in her small plant just a few steps from her kitchen door. She uses hand tools and works on tables that were custom cut to suit her small frame. The recipes for her cheeses are crafted from the traditions she learned from older cheese makers, as well as from her own experience making cheese for nearly twenty years. "It takes some time to understand how to work with the milk," Jodi says. "I rely on chemistry and on intuition." Shepherd's Way cheeses run a gamut of flavors, from the creamy fresh Shepherd's Hope (mild and tangy, firmer than chèvre) to Hidden Falls (a sheep-cow blend with a bloomy rind) to the rich and classic Big Woods Blue to the all-around favorite, Friesago (quite like a good Manchego). The cheeses are widely distributed, and members of the Shepherd's Way CSA benefit from sneak peeks and sample tastes of the new and seasonal cheeses Jodi is crafting.

Shepherd's Way has garnered national attention as a thriving example of Woody Tasch's Slow Money investment model, which connects funders to local food initiatives. Birchwood was an early supporter of Farm Haven, a company that provides means for Shepherd's Way to grow its business in ways good for the land, the animals, and those who love the cheese.

Summer Vegetable Flatbread

Serves 4 to 6

At the Birchwood, we use the same dough for our flatbreads and pizzas. The big difference is that we grill our flatbreads and bake our pizzas. The recipe for our summer flatbread is open to interpretation: vary the vegetables depending on what comes in from the garden or farmers market or CSA delivery.

Birchwood Pizza and Flatbread Dough (page 147)

Garlic Chèvre Mousse (page 34)

4 large radishes, sliced (½ cup)

½ pound yellow squash or zucchini, thinly sliced (1 cup)

3 to 4 ounces arugula (about 3 cups)

4 tablespoons Chili Oil (page 227)

Edible flowers for garnish

Preheat a grill, stovetop pan, or griddle to medium-high. Do not oil the surface. Cut the dough into 4 pieces. On a lightly floured surface, roll out each piece of dough into a 4-inch round. Place each flatbread on the grill and cook without touching until you see bubbles on the surface, about 1 to 2 minutes. Turn the flatbread and continue cooking another 1 to 2 minutes, or until the bread has puffed up.

Spread each flatbread with Garlic Chèvre Mousse. Top the mousse with radishes, sliced squash, and arugula. Drizzle Chili Oil over top, and garnish with edible flowers.

Grilled Pork Chop with Polenta

GF Serves 4

We feature this tender, flavorful pork chop on a bed of soft polenta made with cornmeal that's freshly ground from open-pollinated Riverbend Farm corn. Its true corn flavor shines; it's a perfect match to the meaty chop. Serve with a slice of grilled summer squash or zucchini.

This polenta is also wonderful on its own, topped with shredded sharp cheese and freshly diced tomatoes.

Polenta

4 cups milk	1 cup cornmeal
1 teaspoon salt	2 teaspoons butter, or more to taste

Pork Chop

4 pork loin chops, each about 1 inch thick	Salt and freshly ground black pepper
1 tablespoon minced rosemary	2 tablespoons rice bran oil
	Walnuts for garnish

To make the polenta, put the milk and salt into a large saucepan and bring the milk to a simmer. Whisk in the cornmeal in a slow, steady stream. When the cornmeal is fully absorbed, allow it to simmer over very low heat, stirring occasionally and adding a little water if it's getting too dry, until the polenta is stiff enough to hold a spoon upright and it tastes of sweet corn, about 50 minutes. Swirl in the butter.

To cook the pork chops, pat the chops dry and sprinkle rosemary, salt, and pepper evenly on both sides. Heat the oil in a large, heavy skillet set over high heat. Brown the chops for about 8 minutes, turning them once midway through. Serve the chops on top of the polenta; top with a dollop of Rhubarb Strawberry Jam (page 212) and a sprinkle of walnuts for garnish.

FRESH CORNMEAL IS GROUND FROM DRIED FIELD CORN, and the best-tasting cornmeal comes from nearby fields. Thanks to Riverbend Farm and other local farms, you can get great-tasting cornmeal that is leagues above the quality of any commercial products found on supermarket shelves. Fresh cornmeal is a deep, buttery yellow. It smells like corn, it tastes like corn, and it's slightly moist. Keep it in the refrigerator and use it up quickly (within two weeks) or freeze it.

Riverbend Farm
Delano, Minnesota

Riverbend farmers **Greg and Mary Reynolds** enter Birchwood with a rush of fresh, cool air. Greg beams with ruddy energy; Mary is slender with lively blue eyes and graying blond hair that frames her dewy complexion. This handsome couple founded one of the first significant organic market farms. By introducing us to heirloom and cold-hardy organic varieties of produce, they have done much to shape the way we eat and think about food today. Greg joined the farm-to-school effort early and worked hard with local school systems so kids across the Twin Cities metro area could enjoy salad bars and real baked potatoes at school. An advocate of labeling GMOs from the get-go, he and his crew go to great lengths to save their own seeds.

"The plants we grow from our own seeds always fare much better than any we purchase," he says. "We now have more than twenty-five different tomato varieties, and they all resisted the blight."

Birchwood organizes crop mobs to help plant tomatoes, weed beds, and harvest beans at Riverbend Farm. Joining these crop mobs influences how people (especially kids) understand issues related to food and the environment. "If all my customers visited the farm and learned more about what we do, they would be better customers. It builds a level of involvement or buy-in that you just can't get any other way. It's good for Birchwood's diners, and it's good for us, too," Greg says.

Strawberry and Rhubarb Cornmeal Cobbler Serves 6

Lovely, fresh cornmeal from Riverbend Farm adds a distinctly sweet, corny crunch to the topping. Truth be told, this cobbler is as delicious for breakfast as it is for dessert.

Filling

¼ cup sugar, or more to taste

1 teaspoon unbleached all-purpose flour

Pinch of cloves

1 ½ pounds whole strawberries, hulled and halved (about 6 cups)

2 pounds (about 15 stalks) fresh rhubarb, cut into ½-inch slices (about 6 cups)

Topping

1 cup unbleached all-purpose flour

¼ cup sugar

¼ cup cornmeal

1 tablespoon baking powder

Pinch of salt

3 tablespoons unsalted butter

½ cup buttermilk

Sugar for garnish

Preheat the oven to 400 degrees.

To make the filling, whisk together the sugar, flour, and cloves in a large bowl, and then stir in the strawberries and the rhubarb. Turn the filling into a deep pie dish or six 2-cup ramekins.

To make the topping, stir together the flour, sugar, cornmeal, baking powder, and salt in a large bowl. Using your fingers or a pastry cutter, work in the butter. Slowly work in the buttermilk to make a soft dough. Spoon the topping over the filling and sprinkle it with sugar.

Bake the cobbler until the topping is golden brown and the filling is tender, about 25 minutes. Serve warm with ice cream or at room temperature with fresh whipped cream.

Chocolate Crinkle Cookies

Makes 24 cookies

These old-fashioned cookies are a favorite of Will Allen, the founder of Growing Power and a MacArthur Fellow. Growing Power's urban farming methods, which include aquaponics, vermiculture, and composting, provide oases of fresh, local food in the country's food deserts. I brought these cookies to a Growing Power workshop several years ago and have been dubbed "the Cookie Lady" by Will ever since.

1 ⅔ cups unbleached all-purpose flour

½ cup unsweetened cocoa powder

1 ½ teaspoons baking powder

¼ teaspoon salt

¼ pound (1 stick) unsalted butter, at room temperature

1 ½ cups sugar

2 eggs

1 teaspoon vanilla extract

¼ cup sugar

Preheat the oven to 350 degrees. Cover two baking sheets with parchment paper or grease them lightly with rice bran oil or butter.

In a large bowl, stir together the flour, cocoa powder, baking powder, and salt.

In a separate bowl, beat together the butter and sugar until very creamy, about 3 minutes. Beat in the eggs one at a time; then beat in the vanilla.

Stir the flour mixture into the egg mixture, and beat on low until blended.

Put the sugar in a small bowl.

To shape the cookies, scoop the dough with a tablespoon and roll it into balls between your palms. Roll the balls in the sugar until well covered. Place the balls about 2 inches apart on the prepared cookie sheets.

Bake until the cookies are puffed and cracked, about 10 to 12 minutes. Cool the cookies on racks. Store in airtight containers.

SCORCH

As the heat and humidity intensify, it seems as though someone throws the switch and the tomatoes, potatoes, plump purple eggplants, fat carrots, and string beans appear all at the same time. We rush to keep up, chasing heirloom tomatoes and super sweet corn, trying to catch them at their peak before they turn. Basil, rosemary, and cilantro are everywhere, filling the kitchen with a sweet, green perfume. Squashes are filling out nicely, and the melons are fat, juicy, and sweet. This heat can feel oppressive, and languid appetites need to be teased forth with cold soups, breezy salads, and light crisp vegetable sautés. This is the time to be outside, to cook and eat outdoors, so crank up the grill. Scorch is short, and our menu is long. Dig in!

Sweet Corn Chipotle Coulis

GF Makes about 1 ½ cups

Ready in minutes, this simple condiment is perfect swirled into chilled tomato soup, spooned onto grilled sausages, or served as a dip for chips. It will keep, covered, about five days in the refrigerator.

When fresh corn is in season, we use this coulis in a variety of ways— atop a turkey burger, alongside a hand pie, slathered on an omelet, and, of course, spread on our famous BLT.

1 large ear sweet corn
½ cup heavy cream

1 small chipotle pepper
Salt and freshly ground black pepper

Place the chipotle in a dish of warm water until it has softened, about 5 to 8 minutes. Halve the chipotle, and remove the seeds and veins.

Slice the kernels from the ear of sweet corn. Put the corn kernels, chipotle, and cream into a small saucepan, and bring the cream to a boil. Reduce the heat, and simmer until the corn is very soft. Remove from the heat, and season with salt and pepper to taste. Use an immersion blender, a blender, or a food processor to puree the mixture. Serve warm or at room temperature.

Sweet Corn Wheat Berry Savory Waffle Serves 6 to 8

Come corn season, we work golden sweet kernels into every dish on the menu, starting with our stellar corn-studded savory waffles. We love to serve this waffle topped with a sunny-side up egg, crisp lardoons, toasted hazelnuts, and our fresh Stone Fruit Salsa. If that's too much, simply drizzle the waffle with maple syrup or top it with Sweet Corn Chipotle Coulis (page 54).

This dish is a favorite of Rick Nelson, the *Star Tribune* restaurant critic whose witty, insightful reviews are enjoyed nationwide. The Twin Cities made it on the country's culinary map thanks to Rick's fine work.

COOK'S NOTE

COOK THE WHEAT BERRIES AHEAD OF TIME: Place them in a pot with 2 inches of water. Bring the water to a boil, reduce the heat, and simmer until grain is tender, about 50 to 60 minutes. Drain off the excess water, and refrigerate the grain, covered.

¼ cup wheat berries, cooked (see note)

2 ½ cups unbleached all-purpose flour

½ cup cornmeal

1 tablespoon baking powder

¾ teaspoon baking soda

1 teaspoon salt

3 ¼ cups buttermilk

6 ounces (1 ½ sticks) unsalted butter, melted

3 large eggs, lightly beaten

½ cup corn kernels cut from ½ ear sweet corn

¼ cup chopped basil

1 tablespoon thyme leaves

Rice bran oil or additional melted butter for the waffle iron

Stone Fruit Salsa (page 57)

In a large bowl, stir together the flour, cornmeal, baking powder, baking soda, and salt. Stir in the buttermilk, butter, and eggs to make a thick batter. Fold in the wheat berries, corn kernels, basil, and thyme.

continued on page 57

continued from page 55

Preheat the oven to 200 degrees. Heat up the waffle iron and lightly brush the cooking surfaces with oil. When the waffle iron is ready, pour in 1 cup of batter. Cook until the waffle is lightly browned, about 5 to 6 minutes. Transfer the waffle to a baking sheet and keep it warm, uncovered, in the oven until ready to serve. Repeat with the remaining batter.

Serve each waffle topped with Stone Fruit Salsa. Ramp up the toppings by adding a sunny side-up egg, crisp bacon lardoons, and toasted hazelnuts, or keep it simple and just drizzle on some maple syrup.

FARRO IS ALSO DELICIOUS IN THESE WAFFLES. Simply replace the wheat berries with ½ cup of cooked farro.

Stone Fruit Salsa (V) GF Makes about 4 cups

Make this with any stone fruit available, including plums, pluots, nectarines, and peaches. Be sure to taste the salsa before adding the honey as you don't want it to be too sweet.

6 peaches
1 large sweet onion, chopped
2 inches ginger, grated
  (2 tablespoons)

2 tablespoons rice bran oil
2 tablespoons lime juice
1 tablespoon honey, or more to taste
Salt and freshly ground black pepper

Bring a pot of water to a boil, and fill a bowl with ice water. Score a small X in the bottom of each peach. Put 2 or 3 peaches in the pot of boiling water just until the skins start to split, about 15 seconds. Using a slotted spoon, immediately transfer the peaches to the bowl of ice water. Repeat with the remaining peaches. Peel the peaches, then halve them, remove the pits, and chop the fruit into 1-inch chunks.

In a medium bowl, stir together the peaches, onions, ginger, oil, and lime juice. Taste the salsa, add honey as needed to sweeten, and season to taste with salt and pepper. Serve right away.

Breakfast Black Beans and Rice with Avocado Puree GF Serves 6

Earthy black beans and nutty brown rice capped with a lightly fried or poached egg makes for a complete and comforting start to the day. Serve with tortillas, or a hearty square of cornbread, and a side of grilled summer squash or zucchini.

Skip the eggs for a nutritious, high-protein vegan breakfast.

Black Bean Puree

1 tablespoon rice bran oil

1 large onion, chopped

2 cloves garlic, chopped

½ teaspoon cumin, or more to taste

3 cups cooked black beans (page 67)

2 tablespoons lime juice

Salt and freshly ground black pepper

¼ cup chopped cilantro

Avocado Puree

1 ripe Haas avocado, coarsely chopped

2 tablespoons chopped red onion

2 tablespoons lime juice

¼ cup chopped cilantro leaves

Salt and freshly ground black pepper

1 cup brown rice

Salt

½ cup quinoa

1 tablespoon unsalted butter

6 eggs

12 corn tortillas

Salsa

To make the Black Bean Puree, heat the oil in a large skillet over medium heat. Add the onions and garlic and cook, stirring occasionally, until very soft, about 10 minutes.

Turn the onion mixture into a food processor fitted with a steel blade and add the cumin, cooked black beans, and lime juice. Process until smooth, adding a little water if necessary. Season with salt and pepper to taste. Turn the puree into a bowl, and stir in the cilantro. Taste, and adjust the seasonings.

continued on page 60

continued from page 58

To make the Avocado Puree, put the avocado, onion, and lime juice into a blender and puree until smooth. Scrape the puree into a bowl, and stir in the cilantro. Season to taste with salt and pepper.

To cook the brown rice, put the rice into a saucepan with 3 cups of water and a pinch of salt. Bring to a boil over high heat; then reduce to a simmer, cover the pot, and cook for about 40 minutes. Remove from the heat, and set the covered pot aside for 10 minutes. Uncover the rice, and fluff it with a fork.

Put the quinoa in a fine mesh sieve, and rinse it well with cold water. Scrape the quinoa into a small pot, and cover it with 1 cup of water and a pinch of salt. Bring the water to a boil over high heat; then reduce to a simmer, cover the pot, and cook until the water is absorbed, about 12 to 15 minutes. Remove from the heat, and set the covered pot aside for 5 minutes. Uncover and fluff with a fork. Turn the quinoa into the pot with the brown rice, and toss to combine.

To fry the eggs, melt the butter in a skillet over medium heat. Working in batches, crack two or three eggs into the skillet and cook until the yolks are just set, about 2 to 3 minutes. Transfer the eggs to a plate, and repeat until all the eggs are cooked.

Lightly grill the tortillas or warm them in the oven. To assemble, spoon rice on the plate, then add a tortilla, a scoop of black beans, a lightly fried egg, and a nice scoop of avocado puree. Serve with a side of salsa.

Konstantin Berkovski
Minneapolis, Minnesota

Konstantin Berkovski, a botanist, artist, grower, and philosopher, calls his work a hobby. But in fact, his hobby is the pursuit of beauty. He recently told us, "Eggplant is the most beautiful vegetable. It comes in a great array of forms and shapes, and all of them are stunning." In his travels to Italy, Spain, Malta, the West Coast, and South America, Konstantin searched for seeds that would bring such beauty to his garden and to our plates.

A native of St. Petersburg, Russia, he moved to Minnesota in 1968. His accent carries the authority of struggle, of understanding what it takes to put down roots in foreign soil. Beauty implies persistence and vibrancy, he says. "Our collection of eggplants are Minnesota-loving: they thrive in this short, cold season. Heirloom vegetables are always the best, the result of centuries of selection and refining. Nobody would save seeds from a bad fruit."

Cucumber Basil Gazpacho

(V) GF Serves 4 to 6

The cool, green combo of avocado and cucumber make this smooth, refreshing soup just the thing for a steamy evening.

2 ripe avocadoes, cut into chunks

1 large cucumber, skin on, seeded and cut into chunks

1 cup fresh basil leaves

1 clove garlic

2 green onions, chopped

2 cups corn stock (page 72), or vegetable stock

Juice and zest of 1 lime

Salt and freshly ground black pepper

Put all of the ingredients into a blender and puree, or put the ingredients in a deep bowl and puree with an immersion blender. Taste, and adjust the seasoning. Serve well chilled.

Heirloom Tomato Plate GF Serves 4 to 6

Heirloom tomatoes are grown from open-pollinated plants, which means that wind and insects pollinate the plants rather than humans. Heirloom seeds have been passed down for at least fifty years. Some varieties are sold through seed catalogs, others have been saved and shared among families and neighbors, and others are accidents of crossbreeding in the backyard that create the most exciting varieties. Heirloom tomatoes are a great example of the benefits of biodiversity. When seeds are collected year after year from local varieties, the strongest genetic traits are preserved as those varieties adapt to the climate and develop resistance to diseases and pests.

For this tomato plate, you'll want a nice selection of very ripe heirloom tomatoes that run the gamut of flavors from tart to sweet to mild to tangy.

Sweet Corn Chèvre Mousse

½ cup corn kernels cut from ½ ear of sweet corn

½ cup chèvre

1 tablespoon honey

Salt

Balsamic Reduction

1 cup balsamic vinegar

½ teaspoon brown sugar

3 ½ pounds mixed heirloom tomatoes

Poached Garlic and Honey Vinaigrette (page 238)

To make the Sweet Corn Chèvre Mousse, put the corn kernels into a small skillet and set it over medium heat. Cook, tossing the kernels until they begin to turn brown, about 3 to 4 minutes. Put the roasted corn, chèvre, and honey into a food processor fitted with a steel blade. Process until creamy. Add salt to taste.

To make the Balsamic Reduction, put the vinegar and brown sugar into a small saucepan set over high heat and bring the vinegar to a boil. Reduce the heat, and simmer until the liquid is reduced to ¼ cup, about 10 minutes.

To assemble the plate, slice the tomatoes about ¼ inch thick and cut the cherry tomatoes in half. Arrange the tomatoes on a large platter. Drizzle the vinaigrette over the sliced tomatoes, and follow up with a drizzle of the reduced balsamic vinegar. Garnish with spoonfuls of Sweet Corn Chèvre Mousse.

Spicy Peanut Penne Salad

(V) Serves 4 to 6

This is one of our go-to salads. We vary the ingredients depending on what comes in from the fields. Early in the season, it's sweet peas and radishes; later, it's cherry tomatoes and, of course, lots of corn. As the season progresses, we add carrots, cucumbers, green beans, and finally, cabbages and kale. Keep extra dressing on hand to spark a sandwich or liven up some rice.

8 ounces penne, garganelli, or other pasta

6 tablespoons creamy peanut butter

3 tablespoons rice wine vinegar

2 to 3 tablespoons soy sauce

1 tablespoon brown sugar

2 tablespoons dark sesame oil

1 tablespoon minced fresh garlic

½ cup chopped green onions, white and green parts

2 cups chopped fresh, seasonal vegetables

Salt and freshly ground black pepper

Lettuce leaves

⅓ cup chopped cilantro for garnish

¼ cup unsalted peanuts for garnish

Bring a large pot of lightly salted water to a rolling boil. Drop in the pasta and cook, stirring occasionally, until al dente, about 10 to 12 minutes. Drain.

While the pasta is cooking, whisk together the peanut butter, vinegar, soy sauce, brown sugar, dark sesame oil, garlic, and green onions in a large bowl. Thin the dressing with a little water if it is too thick.

Add the drained pasta and the vegetables to the bowl of dressing, turn to coat with the dressing, and season with salt and pepper to taste. Serve the salad on lettuce leaves, garnished with cilantro and peanuts.

Three Bean Salad with Horseradish Vinaigrette

(V) GF Serves 6 to 8

We developed this simple recipe in collaboration with Minneapolis Public Schools to encourage kids to eat legumes. Many parents told us they were excited to see a Birchwood-inspired salad on their kids' school lunch menu!

2 cups cooked black beans

1 cup cooked kidney beans

½ cup cooked navy beans

1 cup fresh peas, or frozen peas, thawed

¼ pound radishes, diced (about 1 cup)

¼ pound fresh carrots, diced (about 1 cup)

¼ pound baby turnips, peeled and diced (about 1 cup)

¼ cup chopped dill

¼ cup chopped parsley

½ cup Horseradish Vinaigrette (page 233), or more as needed

Toss together the black beans, kidney beans, navy beans, peas, radishes, carrots, turnips, dill, and parsley. Work in the vinaigrette so the ingredients are lightly coated. The salad will store, covered, for up to five days in the refrigerator.

COOK'S NOTE

BIRCHWOOD BEAN BASICS: Soaking beans dramatically reduces the cooking time. There are two ways to do this: overnight or quickly on the stove. For an overnight soak, put the beans into a pot and cover them with at least four times as much water as there are beans. For a quick soak, set the pot of beans and water over high heat and bring the water to a boil. Remove the pot from the heat, and allow the beans to sit, covered, for about one hour.

To cook the beans, drain the soaked beans in a colander and rinse them with cold water. Put the beans into a pot with enough water to cover them by about 3 inches. Set the pot over high heat, and bring the water to a hard boil. Reduce the heat, and skim off the foam that rises to the surface. Simmer the beans until they are soft and creamy inside, about 1 ½ hours depending on the size of the beans and their age. Add a dash of salt to the pot to season the beans when they are almost finished cooking.

Heirloom Tomato Sweet Corn BLT Makes 6 sandwiches

Every year, when tomatoes are at their peak, we make these sandwiches in honor of Tom Taylor, a beloved local food advocate who was instrumental in the early days of the Twin Cities co-op movement. He lived in the Seward neighborhood and was a true friend of the Birchwood —and he loved these BLTs!

1 pound bacon
½ cup Birchwood Aioli (page 239)
 or mayonnaise
1 tablespoon Arugula Basil Pesto
 (page 12)

12 slices toast
12 leaves lettuce
2 large heirloom tomatoes, sliced
Sweet Corn Chipotle Coulis
 (page 54)

Put the bacon in a large skillet, and set it over medium heat. Cook the bacon, turning often, until it is brown and crisped, about 10 to 15 minutes. Drain on paper towels.

Whisk together the aioli and the pesto, and spread it liberally over one side of each slice of toast. Evenly distribute the lettuce leaves and then the tomato slices over 6 of the pieces of toast. Layer on the bacon, followed by Sweet Corn Chipotle Coulis. Top the sandwiches with the remaining 6 slices of toast. Slice diagonally, and serve right away.

Fischer Family Farms Pork
Waseca, Minnesota

Tim **Fischer** of Fischer Family Farms Pork is a fifth-generation pork farmer who raises heritage breeds of hogs and feeds them corn and grains he grows on his farm. The hogs wander outside, and when the weather turns nasty, they snuggle freely together in an enclosed barn with plenty of hay and feed. You can tell the difference in the breed and in the way these hogs are raised because the meat is especially tender and extremely flavorful. "It's the way pork used to taste, is meant to taste, before the industry bred all the flavor out of it by trying to create a pig that could compete with a chicken. I never understood the reason behind the slogan 'the other white meat,'" Tim says. At Birchwood, diners drool over the thick-sliced bacon and the wonderful lardoons.

Photos: Amy Eckert

Sweet Corn Risotto GF Serves 6

This creamy risotto is sparked with bright golden kernels of sweet corn that add crunch and a lovely flavor. If you happen to have a few cherry tomatoes, don't hold back: chop them and toss them, plus a little chopped basil, on top for a bright, flavorful finish. Don't skip making the corn stock; it adds a surprising depth of corn flavor to the dish.

To create a full entrée, serve the risotto with sliced heirloom tomatoes drizzled with Balsamic Reduction (page 64), Chili Oil, crisped coppa or prosciutto, green beans, pistachios, Seed Crackers (page 79), and melon balls.

Corn Stock

2 to 3 ears fresh sweet corn, shucked

6 cups chicken or vegetable stock

Risotto

3 tablespoons unsalted butter or extra-virgin olive oil

1 medium onion, chopped

1 ½ cups Arborio rice

½ cup dry white wine

½ cup freshly grated Parmesan cheese

Salt and freshly ground black pepper

4 tablespoons Chili Oil (page 227)

To make the Corn Stock, slice the kernels from the cobs and set the kernels aside. Put the corncobs and the chicken stock into a medium saucepan set over medium heat. Bring the stock to a simmer; then reduce the heat to low. Simmer the stock for 15 to 20 minutes, and discard the cobs. Reduce the heat to low to keep the stock warm.

To make the risotto, melt the butter in a large saucepan. Add the onion and cook, stirring, over moderately high heat until it is softened, about 2 minutes. Add the rice and cook, stirring, until the rice is opaque, about 3 minutes. Add the wine and cook, stirring, until the wine is completely absorbed, about 1 minute.

Reduce the heat to medium, add 1 cup of the warm stock, and cook, stirring, until the stock is nearly absorbed. Continue adding the stock 1 cup at a time, stirring until it is absorbed. After about half of the stock has been added, stir in the corn kernels, and then continue adding the stock a cup at a time. The rice is done when it's al dente and creamy, about 25 minutes total. Stir in the cheese. Season with salt and pepper and a drizzle of Chili Oil.

Grilled Corn with Crème Fraîche

GF Serves 6

Grilling corn draws all the wonderful sugars to the surface and gives the kernels a smoky-sweet crunch. Along with butter, we like to slather grilled corn with crème fraîche and a squirt of lime juice.

6 plump ears of sweet corn
Salt and freshly ground black pepper

2 limes, cut into quarters
1 cup crème fraîche

Heat the grill to medium. Shuck the corn and place it on the grill. Roll the corn frequently so it cooks evenly. Remove the corn from the grill when it is slightly charred and the kernels are soft, about 5 minutes. Season the corn with salt and pepper, lime juice, and a dollop of crème fraîche. Serve lime wedges on the side.

Crème Fraîche Makes 2 cups

Crème fraîche is tangier and richer tasting than fresh cream and a bit thicker. A little goes a long way to enrich sauces and soups. Blended with fresh herbs and a dash of lemon or lime, it's lovely on grilled vegetables, especially grilled corn.

2 tablespoons cultured buttermilk
Pinch of salt

2 cups heavy cream

Pour the buttermilk and the cream into a clean glass jar. Cover the jar with a clean dishcloth or cheesecloth. Let the cream stand at room temperature for 24 hours, or until thickened. Stir, and season with a pinch of salt. Refrigerate for at least a day before using. Crème fraîche will keep in the refrigerator for about two weeks.

Veggie Baba Ghanoush Pizza

(V) Serves 4 to 6

With eggplant at its peak, we can't resist enjoying it in all its many forms. This lush, vegan baba ghanoush provides a rich base for bright cherry tomatoes and refreshing cucumbers. Save leftover baba ghanoush for a dip or to spread on sandwiches and in pita pockets.

Baba Ghanoush

2 pounds eggplants, each cut in half lengthwise

¼ cup extra-virgin olive oil

¼ cup tahini

3 tablespoons lemon juice

1 clove garlic, minced

Pizza

Cornmeal for dusting the pan

Birchwood Pizza and Flatbread Dough (page 147)

1 to 2 cups cherry tomatoes, halved

1 bunch green onions, white and green parts thinly sliced (1 cup)

½ cup diced red bell pepper

¼ cup chopped cilantro

¼ cup chopped basil

Make the Baba Ghanoush. Preheat the oven to 350 degrees. Generously oil a baking sheet, and place the eggplants cut-side down on the sheet. Roast the eggplants until they are very soft, about 45 minutes to 1 hour. Using a spoon, scoop out the pulp into a strainer set over a bowl, and let the excess liquid drain for about 30 minutes. Put the drained eggplant into a food processor fitted with a steel blade (or into a blender), and puree the eggplant with the olive oil, tahini, lemon juice, and garlic.

Meanwhile, prepare the crust. Raise the oven temperature to 425 degrees. Dust a pizza peel or a rimless baking sheet with cornmeal or a little flour.

On a lightly floured surface, roll out the dough into a 9- to 10-inch circle and place it on the pizza peel. Gently shake the peel back and forth to make sure the crust is not sticking; then transfer the crust to the oven rack. Bake the crust until it is firm and crusty brown, about 10 to 15 minutes.

To assemble the pizza, spread the baba ghanoush evenly over the baked pizza crust and arrange the tomatoes, green onions, and red bell pepper on top of the baba ghanoush. Garnish with chopped cilantro and basil.

Black Bean Quinoa Burger

(V) GF Serves 4 to 6

This award-winning burger is hearty enough to join the ranks at the next cookout, and no one will be asking "Where's the beef?" Make a few extra patties to keep in the freezer for a busy weeknight.

Skip the bun and serve this on a plate of greens for a light, fresh entrée or a starter course. If you want to kick up the spice, Roasted Jalapeño Aioli (page 239) adds a lush heat!

¼ cup fine cornmeal

2 tablespoons potato starch

2 teaspoons cumin

2 teaspoons coriander

2 teaspoons freshly ground black pepper

1 teaspoon salt

1 cup black beans, cooked until mushy and drained

1 russet potato, roasted until soft and peeled

¼ cup quinoa, steeped in boiling water for 5 minutes and drained

¼ cup garlic oil (see page 238)

Rice bran oil for the skillet

In a small bowl, stir together the cornmeal, potato starch, cumin, coriander, pepper, and salt.

In a food processor fitted with a steel blade, puree the mushy beans and potato. Pulse in the quinoa, garlic oil, and the cornmeal mixture. The mixture should be slightly chunky.

Film a heavy skillet with oil and set it over medium-high heat. Cook a tablespoon of the burger mix, taste it, and adjust the seasoning.

Form the mixture into patties, and cook them over medium-high heat until they are nicely browned on one side, about 5 minutes. Turn carefully, and cook the other side until firm and browned.

Serve the burgers topped with creamy Avocado Chèvre Mousse (page 78) and plenty of thick tomato slices.

continued on page 78

continued from page 77

Avocado Chèvre Mousse GF Makes about 1 cup

Serve the Black Bean Quinoa Burger, or any burger, topped with a dollop of this sumptuous mousse. It's also lovely spooned over sliced tomatoes or used as a sandwich spread.

¼ cup heavy cream

2 ounces chèvre

½ cup Avocado Puree (page 58)

1 tablespoon chopped chives

Salt and freshly ground black pepper

In the bowl of a stand mixer, whip the cream until it holds stiff peaks; then add the chèvre. Remove the bowl from the mixer, and fold in the avocado puree and chives. Season to taste with salt and black pepper.

Seed Crackers (V) Makes about 40 crackers

These light, crisp crackers are wonderful spread with Red Pepper Chickpea Puree (page 22), on a cheese plate, or with soup and Sweet Corn Risotto (page 72).

1 cup high-gluten flour (see note)
1 cup unbleached all-purpose flour
2 tablespoons flax seeds
¼ cup white sesame seeds
¼ cup black sesame seeds

1 teaspoon salt
½ teaspoon baking powder
¼ cup rice bran oil
½ to ¾ cup water
Flaked salt

Preheat the oven to 300 degrees. Lightly grease two baking sheets or line them with parchment paper.

In a large bowl, combine the flours, seeds, salt, and baking powder. Stir in the oil and water, and mix to create a stiff dough. Divide the dough in half. On a lightly floured countertop, using a lightly floured rolling pin, roll out each portion of dough as thin as possible. Cut the rolled-out dough into large squares or diamonds, and transfer them onto the prepared baking sheets. Spritz lightly with water, and sprinkle on a little flaked salt. Bake until nice and crispy, about 20 to 25 minutes. Remove from the oven, and transfer the crackers to a rack to cool.

COOK'S NOTE

HIGH-GLUTEN FLOUR is available in the bulk section of most co-ops.

Stone Fruit Maple Quinoa Crisp

(V) GF Serves 6 to 8

This is the kind of old-fashioned dessert I remember making with my great-grandma during those summer visits in Georgia. Together, we would gather blueberries and raspberries and pick low-hanging peaches.

The Birchwood take on this favorite is crunchy and nutritious. Maple syrup adds flavor while keeping the dessert from being overly sweet.

2 pounds stone fruit (apricots, plums, nectarines, peaches), pitted and cut into large dice (about 4 cups)

½ cup maple syrup

2 cups rolled oats

¼ cup quinoa

1 teaspoon cinnamon

1 teaspoon vanilla extract

¼ cup rice bran oil

Preheat the oven to 350 degrees. In a medium bowl, mix the fruit with ¼ cup of the maple syrup. Turn the fruit into a deep 9-inch-square baking dish.

In a separate bowl, stir together the oats, quinoa, cinnamon, vanilla, remaining maple syrup, and oil. Distribute the topping over the fruit. Bake until the top is toasty and golden and the fruit is bubbly, about 25 to 30 minutes.

Blueberry Muffins (V) Makes 12 muffins

These light muffins have a tender crumb and lively blueberry flavor. Great for breakfast, they are terrific with afternoon coffee and tea too.

2 cups unbleached all-purpose flour
2 teaspoons baking powder
½ teaspoon salt
⅔ cup packed light brown sugar
½ cup plain soy milk yogurt or
   almond milk yogurt

⅓ cup unsweetened almond or
   coconut milk
⅓ cup rice bran oil
¼ cup unsweetened applesauce
1 teaspoon vanilla extract
2 cups fresh blueberries
2 tablespoons maple sugar

Preheat the oven to 350 degrees. Line a 12-muffin tin with paper liners or lightly coat the cups with rice bran oil.

In a large bowl, whisk together the flour, baking powder, and salt. In a medium bowl, whisk together the brown sugar, yogurt, milk, oil, applesauce, and vanilla.

Gently fold the wet mixture into the dry mixture; then fold in the blueberries. Divide the batter evenly among the muffin cups. Sprinkle the tops with maple sugar. Bake until a tester inserted in the center comes out clean, about 20 to 24 minutes. Let the muffins cool on a rack before removing them from the pan.

AUTUMN

As days cool and shadows lengthen, we smell the change in the air. It's back to school, off to pick apples; squash and pumpkins hang heavy on their vines. Nature accommodates our busy schedules with a harvest that does not require our immediate attention, quite different from the delicate tomatoes and sugary sweet corn of Scorch. These vegetables wait patiently on the counter or in the crisper until we can whip up curries and soups and stews. We rush to get the garden in the jar, putting up pickles, preserves, jams, and jellies to spark wintery meals. It's cider season! Thanks to our orchards, we have much to choose from, both sweet and hard ciders for sipping and for sparking braises, soups, and sauces. Harvest festivals, Oktoberfest, and Halloween remind us to pause in gratitude for a bountiful harvest and stocked pantries.

Cinnamon Apple Farro Pancakes

Serves 6 to 8

Farro adds a nutty flavor and texture to our light, sweet pancakes shot through with bits of tangy sweet apple. Serve the pancakes with sautéed apples and candied nuts.

2 cups unbleached all-purpose flour

1 tablespoon baking powder

½ teaspoon salt

1 tablespoon sugar

2 eggs, separated

1 cup milk

½ cup yogurt

2 tablespoons butter, melted

2 medium tart apples, peeled, cored, and diced, ½ cup reserved for topping

¼ cup farro, cooked (see note)

Rice bran oil for cooking

1 tablespoon butter

Honey-Roasted Almonds (page 35)

Apple Cinnamon Butter (page 86)

Maple syrup

Preheat the oven to 200 degrees.

In a large bowl, stir together the flour, baking powder, salt, and sugar.

In a separate bowl, whip the egg whites until they hold soft peaks.

In a third bowl, whisk together the egg yolks, milk, yogurt, and melted butter. Turn this mixture into the dry ingredients, and stir to combine. Fold in the egg whites and then the chopped apples and cooked farro.

Lightly film a large skillet or griddle with oil, and set it over medium-high heat. Pour about ¼ cup of batter per pancake onto the griddle, and cook until the bottoms are browned, about 2 to 4 minutes. Flip the pancakes, and continue cooking another 2 to 4 minutes. Transfer the pancakes to a baking sheet and hold, uncovered, in the warm oven until ready to serve.

Melt the butter in a small skillet set over medium heat, and sauté the reserved chopped apples until they are soft and lightly browned.

Serve the pancakes topped with sautéed apples, a dab of Apple Cinnamon Butter, chopped Honey-Roasted Almonds, and a drizzle of maple syrup.

AT THE BIRCHWOOD, WE USE KERNZA IN THIS RECIPE.

It's a perennial wheatgrass selectively bred by the Land Institute in Kansas, where Wes Jackson and Don Wyse (from the University of Minnesota) have been growing experimental crops that do not require tilling or chemical inputs. This means less erosion and far fewer fertilizers and pesticides. Kernza has higher levels of folate, betaine, calcium, lutein, omega-3 fatty acids, fiber, selenium, and vitamin B6 than commercially grown varieties of wheat. Because Kernza is an experimental grain and not yet widely available, use farro, barley, or brown rice in this recipe.

To cook farro, put the desired amount of farro in a pot and cover it with 1 to 2 inches of water. Bring the water to a boil, reduce the heat, and simmer until the grain is tender, about 15 to 20 minutes. Drain off any excess water.

Seasoned Butter GF Makes ½ to 1 cup

Flavored butters work wonders in the kitchen. Spread sweet and spicy butters on pancakes and waffles, and toss savory butters with pasta and rice. Seasoned butters freeze beautifully.

Apple Cinnamon Butter

¼ pound (1 stick) unsalted butter, at room temperature

1 teaspoon cinnamon

1 small apple, peeled, cored, and finely chopped (about ½ cup)

Salt

In a small bowl, beat the butter with a wooden spoon until it's soft. Stir in the cinnamon and the chopped apple, and season to taste with salt.

Radish Butter

This butter is gorgeous spread on thinly sliced rye or pumpernickel and topped with a few specks of coarse salt. Use it to top grilled trout or to garnish freshly steamed peas.

¼ pound radishes, trimmed and minced

¼ pound (1 stick) unsalted butter, at room temperature

¼ cup minced green onions

Grated zest of 1 lemon

Salt and freshly ground black pepper

Put the minced radishes into a fine mesh strainer, and press to remove any excess liquid. Place the butter in a medium bowl. Add the radishes, green onions, and lemon zest, and use a spatula to work the radishes, onions, and lemon zest into the butter. Season to taste with salt and pepper. Covered, the butter will keep in the refrigerator for about 3 to 4 days.

continued on page 88

continued from page 86

Cilantro Butter

¼ pound (1 stick) unsalted butter,
  at room temperature
¼ cup chopped fresh cilantro

1 tablespoon lime juice
Salt and freshly ground black pepper

Put the butter, cilantro, and lime juice into a food processor fitted with a steel blade. Process until thoroughly combined. Season to taste with salt and pepper.

Lemon Pepita Butter

Serve this butter with waffles, on toast, or swirled into rice.

½ pound (2 sticks) unsalted butter,
  at room temperature
¼ cup chopped toasted pepitas

Grated zest and juice of 1 lemon
Salt and freshly ground pepper

Put all of the ingredients into a bowl, and work them together with a spatula.

Mint Honey Butter

This butter is terrific slathered onto blueberry muffins, drizzled over waffles, and spread on toast.

½ pound (2 sticks) unsalted butter,
  at room temperature
¼ cup mint leaves

2 tablespoons honey
Salt

In a small bowl, beat the butter with a wooden spoon, and work in the mint leaves and honey. Season to taste with salt.

Autumn Vegetable Quiche

Serves 6 to 8

Great for brunch or a simple light supper, this is a quiche for all seasons. We vary the veggies depending on what's in the walk-in and make use of extra roasted vegetables and the odds and ends of good cheese. We love the subtle earthiness that Shepherd's Way Friesago lends this quiche.

Basic Pastry Crust (page 5)

1 small fennel bulb, trimmed and diced into ½-inch cubes

½ pound Brussels sprouts, sliced ½ inch thick (1 cup)

½ small head cauliflower, florets broken into ½-inch pieces (1 cup)

2 tablespoons rice bran oil

5 large eggs

½ cup heavy cream

½ cup whole milk

¼ teaspoon salt

⅛ teaspoon freshly ground black pepper

1 cup shredded cheddar cheese

COOK'S NOTE

IT'S A GOOD IDEA TO SLIGHTLY PREBAKE A CRUST before adding any kind of filling. This helps to keep the crust from getting soggy.

Preheat the oven to 425 degrees. Roll out the pastry dough, and fit it into a deep 9-inch pie pan. Line the crust with parchment paper, and weight it with pie weights, dried beans, or rice. Bake the crust about 12 minutes. Remove the pie weights and parchment paper, and set the crust aside.

In a large bowl, toss the fennel, Brussels sprouts, and cauliflower with the oil, and then spread the vegetables on a baking sheet. Roast the vegetables, shaking the pan occasionally, until they are nicely crisped on the outside and tender, about 15 to 20 minutes.

Reduce the oven temperature to 325 degrees.

In a large bowl, whisk together the eggs, cream, milk, salt, and pepper, and then stir in half of the cheese. Stir in the roasted vegetables. Place the pan with the baked crust on a rimmed baking sheet, and carefully pour the egg mixture into the crust. Top with the remaining cheese. Carefully transfer the baking sheet to the oven, and bake until the mixture is just set but still moist, about 40 minutes. The quiche should jiggle a little in the middle. Cool several minutes on a wire rack, and serve at room temperature.

Chicken Spaetzle Soup Serves 6 to 8

Birchwood Soup of the Month was one of the most popular incentives in our 2013 Kickstarter campaign. Thanks to our community of supporters, and their love of our soup, we raised the funds to remodel our kitchen and expand our sunny space.

Chicken Spaetzle Soup is homey and reliable, a customer favorite. The daughter of one of our customers once said, "Mom, I need to feel better. Please go get me some Birchwood chicken soup."

Soup

2 pounds boneless, skinless chicken thighs

3 tablespoons rice bran oil

2 yellow onions, diced

2 carrots, diced

4 celery stalks, chopped

1 turnip, peeled and diced

2 cloves garlic, chopped

½ cup white wine

2 tablespoons tamari

2 tablespoons lemon juice

5 to 6 cups chicken stock

¼ cup chopped parsley, plus extra for garnish

1 tablespoon thyme leaves

2 teaspoons chopped rosemary

½ bay leaf

Salt and freshly ground black pepper

Spaetzle

2 cups unbleached all-purpose flour

2 eggs

½ cup heavy cream

¼ cup milk

¼ teaspoon salt

¼ teaspoon freshly ground black pepper

⅛ teaspoon nutmeg

Preheat the oven to 350 degrees. Coat the chicken with about 1 tablespoon of the oil, and roast until the chicken is cooked through and the juices run clear, about 20 to 25 minutes. Allow to cool, and then cut into ½-inch pieces.

continued on page 92

continued from page 90

In a large, deep pot, heat the remaining 2 tablespoons of oil over high heat, and sauté the onions, carrots, celery, turnips, and garlic until the vegetables soften and begin to brown, about 5 minutes. Stir in the wine, tamari, lemon juice, stock, parsley, thyme, rosemary, and bay leaf, and bring to a boil. Reduce the heat, and simmer about 5 minutes. Season to taste with salt and pepper.

To make the spaetzle, put the flour, eggs, cream, milk, salt, pepper, and nutmeg in a medium bowl and mix until the dough is smooth. Rinse a potato ricer or a colander in cold water. Working in batches, press ¼ cup of the dough through the ricer directly into the simmering soup. Simmer the spaetzle for about 2 minutes. Serve the soup garnished with chopped parsley.

Maple Squash Soup (V) GF Serves 4 to 6

Butternut squash makes a lush, silky base for this soup, thus eliminating the need for cream. Unlike ribbed acorn squash or tough Hubbard squash, smooth-skinned butternut squash is relatively easy to peel. We garnish this soup with spicy pepitas.

2 tablespoons rice bran oil

1 medium onion, chopped

2 pounds butternut squash, peeled, seeded, and cut into ½-inch pieces

1 cup apple cider

2 cups vegetable stock or water

1 cup coconut milk

2 tablespoons maple syrup

Salt and freshly ground black pepper

Microgreens

Spiced pepitas (see note)

TO MAKE SPICED PEPITAS: Rinse about 1 cup of squash seeds and remove all the strings. Spread the seeds on paper towels to dry thoroughly. Toss the dry seeds with just enough oil to coat, and roast them in a 325-degree oven until golden, about 15 minutes. While the seeds are still warm, sprinkle them with a little ground coriander, salt, black pepper, and a pinch of cayenne, and stir. Return the pepitas to the oven for about a minute. Cool before storing in an airtight container.

Heat the oil in a heavy saucepan over low heat, and sauté the onion, stirring, until it's tender but not browned, about 5 minutes.

Add the squash, apple cider, and stock. Simmer until the squash is very tender, about 20 minutes. Stir in the coconut milk and the maple syrup. Working in batches, puree the soup in a blender. Return the soup to the pot, adding more liquid as desired, season with salt and pepper, and heat through. Serve garnished with microgreens and spiced pepitas.

Apple and Alemar Salad with Cranberry Vinaigrette GF Serves 4 to 6

Our friend Keith Adams of Alemar Cheese Company (Mankato, Minnesota) makes Bent River, an award-winning Camembert-style cheese, using organic, grass-fed milk from local farms. "In this region, milk, especially from a single source, is the best expression of terroir," he says. "The cheese I make changes with the season, depending on the weather and the grass the cows eat, and it's what makes this place so special."

This salad—a toss of heritage apples, Bent River cheese, red onions, candied walnuts, and cranberry vinaigrette—is the essence of fall.

½ pound lardoons or bacon, cut into 2-inch pieces

5 to 6 ounces mixed greens

4 to 6 small wedges Bent River or Camembert cheese

2 tart apples, such as Haralson or Honeycrisp, cored and cut into wedges

1 small red onion, thinly sliced

½ cup Honey-Roasted Walnuts (page 35)

¼ cup Cranberry Vinaigrette (page 233)

In a large skillet set over medium heat, fry the lardoons until crisp, turning occasionally, about 5 to 8 minutes. Drain the lardoons on paper towels.

Put the lettuce on individual plates or a large serving platter, and then scatter the lardoons over the lettuce. Arrange the cheese, apples, and onions on the plate, and scatter the walnuts over top. Drizzle the dressing over the salad.

Featherstone Farm
Rushford, Minnesota

Nestled in the fertile valley of the Minnesota River bluffs, in a landscape of steep bluffs and rolling hillsides, Featherstone Farm lies two hours southeast of the Twin Cities along the Mississippi River Valley. Untouched by glacial drift, this area lacks the sedimentary layers that typify the rest of the region. Bordered by deep woods, Featherstone's fields stretch over 250 acres where the morning fog hugs the valley. Who knew there could be so many shades of green? Pale lettuces, emerald kale, lacy carrot tops, rows of cabbages contribute to the palette. Farmer **Jack Hedin**'s fields are sculpted into the hillsides in curving patterns that capture the increasingly heavy rains and prevent runoff, and in the sun they wave with life.

Jack is a rangy man with curly gray hair whose inspiration comes from his grandfather, A.P. Anderson. Featherstone is the name of the township in Goodhue County where A.P. homesteaded in the nineteenth century. By the early 1920s, he had expanded the farm to five hundred acres and was practicing conservation tillage methods employed by many organic and conventional farmers today. "A.P. saw the destructiveness

of pre-dust bowl agriculture in the area. He was keenly sensitive to the richness and diversity of the high grasses and woodlands that he had helped to plow up, chop down, and grub out in his youth. He planted tens of thousands of trees and shrubs on his farm to replace what he had destroyed," Jack says. Featherstone's practices are guided by the wisdom in A.P.'s self-published memoir, *The Seventh Reader*.

Jack's editorials in the *New York Times* about farming issues and climate change inspired me to step up and step out, to advocate for the values represented in Birchwood's Good Real Food—respect for the farmers, respect for the animals, respect for the planet.

Cherry Hazelnut Turkey Salad

GF Serve 6 to 8

This is one of our favorite entrée salads. Easily doubled, it's perfect on a luncheon buffet and makes delicious use of leftover turkey.

3 cups diced roasted turkey

1 cup finely chopped celery

2 tablespoons chopped white onion

2 tablespoons chopped tarragon

¼ cup chopped toasted hazelnuts
  (see note)

½ cup dried cherries, chopped

1 tablespoon white wine vinegar

⅔ cup mayonnaise

1 teaspoon whole-grain mustard

1 teaspoon lemon juice

Salt and freshly ground black pepper

Put the turkey, celery, onion, 1 tablespoon of the tarragon, hazelnuts, and cherries in a large bowl. Toss in the vinegar, and stir to combine.

In a small bowl, whisk together the mayonnaise, mustard, remaining tarragon, and lemon juice, and season to taste with salt and pepper. Pour the dressing onto the salad, and toss to coat.

COOK'S NOTE

TO TOAST NUTS: Lightly coat them in oil and spread them on a baking sheet. Toast the nuts in a 350-degree oven until they are just slightly brown and toasty, about 8 to 10 minutes. You'll know they are ready by their scent. Cool before chopping or using in a recipe.

To remove the skins from toasted hazelnuts, roll the warm toasted nuts in a clean dishtowel. The skins will flake right off.

Limousin Beef Brisket with Maple Squash Mash and Aronia Berry Coulis GF Serves 6 to 8

Serve the brisket on Maple Squash Mash and garnish it with roasted vegetables and toasted hazelnuts for a beautiful dish. This recipe is really a two for one: braise the roast for supper, and enjoy leftovers in hearty sandwiches and on pizzas. Hang on to the braising juices to use as a base for chili or soup. The meat freezes beautifully.

1 tablespoon rice bran oil
1 small beef brisket (about 3 pounds)
Salt and lots of freshly ground black pepper

3 tablespoons unsalted butter
1 medium onion, minced
2 cloves minced garlic
½ cup dark beer
4 cups beef or vegetable stock

Preheat the oven to 325 degrees. Film a large Dutch oven or flame-proof casserole with the oil, and set it over medium-high heat. Season the beef with salt and pepper; then sear it on all sides until well browned, about 5 minutes per side. Transfer the brisket to a platter.

Wipe out the pan with paper towels, then add the butter and set the pan over medium heat. Add the onions, and cook until they are golden and soft, about 10 minutes. Stir in the garlic, and then add the beer and the stock, scraping up any bits that have clung to the bottom. Season with salt and pepper, and then return the beef to the pot.

Cover the pot and place it in the oven. Cook, turning the meat about every 30 minutes, until very tender, about 3 to 4 hours. When the meat is done, place it on a platter. Set the pot over high heat, bring the liquid to a boil, and reduce until the pan juices have thickened.

continued on page 101

continued from page 99

Carve the brisket into ½-inch slices, and serve them on a bed of Maple Squash Mash. Drizzle thickened pan juices and Aronia Berry Coulis over top.

Maple Squash Mash GF Serves 4 to 6

You can substitute sweet potatoes for the squash.

Here's the perfect side to the brisket. It also makes a wonderful base for soup with the addition of a little stock. This mash keeps several days in the refrigerator or can be frozen, so don't hesitate to double the recipe and store some of the mash for later uses.

2 ½ to 3 pounds acorn, red kuri, or butternut squash, halved and seeded

¼ cup maple syrup, or more to taste

1 tablespoon unsalted butter, at room temperature

2 tablespoons heavy cream or milk

Salt and freshly ground black pepper

Preheat the oven to 350 degrees. Lay a square of parchment paper on a baking sheet. Place the squash cut-side down on the parchment paper. Roast until the squash is very tender, about 1 hour. Allow the squash to cool a little; then scoop out the flesh and put it in a medium bowl. Stir in the maple syrup, butter, and cream, and season to taste with salt and pepper. Serve warm.

Aronia Berry Coulis (V) GF Makes 1 cup

2 cups aronia berries

¼ cup water

¼ cup red wine vinegar

3 tablespoons maple syrup

Pinch of sugar

⅓ cup brown sugar

Salt and freshly ground black pepper

Put all of the ingredients into a medium saucepan, and bring the mixture to a boil. Reduce the heat, and simmer until the berries are very soft and the mixture becomes soft and jammy, about 10 minutes. Pour the sauce into a blender and puree it. Press the sauce through a fine mesh sieve or a chinois, and season it to taste with salt and pepper.

Braised Beef Pizza Serves 4 to 6

Pizza is one of our favorite uses for leftover beef brisket or braised beef. It adds oomph to a spicy topping of peppers, onions, and sharp cheddar cheese—like a Philly Beef sandwich on a pizza crust.

Cornmeal for dusting the pan

Birchwood Pizza and Flatbread Dough (page 147)

2 tablespoons Anaheim Chili Sauce (page 240)

1 mild chili pepper (such as Anaheim), seeded, veined, and chopped

½ cup shredded Limousin Beef Brisket (page 99) or other braised beef

½ cup crumbled Big Woods Blue or sharp cheddar cheese

Preheat the oven to 425 degrees. Dust a pizza peel or a rimless baking sheet with cornmeal or a little flour. On a lightly floured surface, roll out the dough into a 9- to 10-inch circle; then place it on the pizza peel.

Spread the Anaheim Chili Sauce over the dough; then distribute the chili pepper, brisket, and blue cheese on top. Gently shake the peel back and forth to make sure the crust is not sticking; then transfer the crust to the oven rack. Bake until the cheese is bubbly, about 20 minutes.

Limousin Beef Sandwich with Roasted Pear Mayo Serves 4 to 6

Braised beef makes a fabulous sandwich, especially when paired with Roasted Pear Mayo. Be sure to slice the beef extra thin.

Roasted Pear Mayo

1 pear, peeled, halved, and cored

1 cup Birchwood Aioli (page 239) or mayonnaise

1 clove garlic, minced

Salt and freshly ground black pepper

Sandwich

1 pound Limousin Beef Brisket (page 99) or other braised beef

Sliced hearty bread, such as multigrain or rye

1 small head butter lettuce, rinsed and dried

1 small red onion, very thinly sliced

For the Roasted Pear Mayo, preheat the oven to 350 degrees. Line a small baking sheet with parchment paper. Lay the pear halves cut-side down on the parchment paper. Roast until very soft, about 55 to 60 minutes.

Puree the pear, aioli, and garlic in a food processor fitted with a steel blade. Season to taste with salt and pepper.

To make the sandwiches, slice the beef very thin. Spread about 1 tablespoon of the Roasted Pear Mayo on each slice of bread. Line the bread with lettuce, add some onions, and pile on about 3 to 4 ounces of beef per sandwich.

Peterson Limousin Beef
Osceola, Wisconsin

Limousin is a handsome breed of cattle that originated in the Marche and Limoges regions of France. The beef is flavorful yet lean and tender, so delicious that French chefs kept it a secret for years. At the Petersons' ranch in Osceola, these cattle are raised on grass near the St. Croix River Valley. Seven Petersons work together in their family operation and collaborate with a local meat processor, then distribute their beef to local restaurants and retail outlets. At a "We Heart Community Dinner" at Birchwood, where we invite guests to dine with a dozen of our farmers, Wayne Peterson raised his glass in a toast to Birchwood and, in a voice filled with emotion, said, "This is the first time I've experienced so many people in one room enjoying our beef, enjoying each other's company. It means so much to our family to be a part of this community."

Apple Walnut Scones Makes 4 to 6 scones

There's a trick to making scones: don't overmix. We give approximate amounts of cream here, but add it slowly and sparingly. You want just enough for the flour to come together into a stiff, soft dough. Scones are best served warm.

2 cups unbleached all-purpose flour

1 tablespoon baking powder

2 tablespoons sugar, plus extra for topping

1 teaspoon fine salt

1 teaspoon cinnamon

1 ½ cups heavy cream

½ teaspoon vanilla extract

1 small apple, peeled, cored, and finely chopped (½ cup)

2 tablespoons finely chopped toasted walnuts (page 98)

Preheat the oven to 400 degrees. Line a baking sheet with parchment paper.

In a medium bowl, toss together the flour, baking powder, sugar, salt, and cinnamon.

In a small bowl, whisk together the cream and vanilla. Make a well in the center of the flour mixture and slowly, sparingly, add the cream and vanilla. Stir until a sticky, stiff dough forms; then work in the apples and walnuts.

Turn the dough out onto a lightly floured surface and pat it into a 5-inch round. Transfer the round to the baking sheet, and lightly brush it with a little cream. Sprinkle the dough with a little sugar. Score into quarters or sixths, making ¼-inch deep cuts with a sharp knife.

Bake until golden, about 20 to 25 minutes. Transfer the scones to a rack to cool a bit. Break the scones along the score marks, and serve them while they are still warm.

Carmelitas Makes about 32 small bars

Bar none, these are great old-fashioned bars, oozing with caramel, dense with dark chocolate. We won't pretend they're good for you, but they are really good!

2 cups unbleached all-purpose flour

2 cups rolled oats

1 ½ cups firmly packed brown sugar

1 teaspoon baking soda

½ teaspoon salt

1 ¼ cups (2 ½ sticks) unsalted butter, at room temperature

1 cup caramels

1 cup semisweet or bittersweet chocolate pieces

½ cup chopped nuts

Preheat the oven to 350 degrees. Line a 9 × 13-inch pan with parchment paper, allowing about 1 inch of the parchment paper to rise above the sides.

In a large mixing bowl, stir together the flour, oats, brown sugar, baking soda, salt, and butter until combined and crumbly. Set aside half of the mixture (about 3 cups) for the topping. Press the remaining crumb mixture into the bottom of the prepared pan and bake until slightly firm and golden, about 10 minutes.

In a small saucepan, melt the caramels over very low heat, stirring until smooth.

Scatter the chocolate pieces over the crust; then pour the melted caramel over the chocolate.

Crumble the remaining oatmeal mixture over the caramel layer, and scatter the nuts over top. Bake until golden brown, about 20 to 30 minutes. Cool the bars on a wire rack; then use the parchment paper to lift the bars out of the pan. Cut into small bars.

DUSK

Fall has fallen all around; the trees are bare, and willows glow in the late sun. As the winds rattle the windows and clouds hang low and heavy with snow, let's cozy in with bowls of warming soups, fragrant stews, bold curries, and robust braises seasoned with the bracing notes of rosemary and dusty sage. Cranberries brighten roasts and spark breads, cookies, and tarts with an assertive tang. Bread baking, pie making, and the floury fun of decorating cookies fill the house with warm, spicy scents and bring the holidays to life. Thanksgiving turkey, roast beef, and pork are the hallmarks of our feasts, giving substance to grain salads, pizzas, soups, and stews. What's better than turning the odds and ends from a beloved meal into another homey dish? Light the fire, relax, invite friends in to savor the delights of Dusk.

Bacon Blueberry Black Currant Oatmeal GF Serves 4 to 6

This hearty breakfast of local steel cut oats topped with Blueberry Black Currant Jam gets a sweet and spicy hit from maple syrup and sambal. The recipe for this dish was featured in the Minnesota Cooks calendar published by the Minnesota Farmers Union. We use steel cut oats because they are a hearty match for the bacon, but old-fashioned rolled oats will also work nicely.

4 to 6 ounces bacon, cut into
¼-inch pieces
1 cup steel cut oats
3 cups water
¼ cup maple syrup

1 tablespoon sambal
½ cup Blueberry Black Currant Jam
(page 215)
Pistachios

In a large skillet set over medium-low heat, cook the bacon, stirring occasionally, until it is deep golden brown and crisp, about 5 to 8 minutes. Using a slotted spoon, transfer the bacon to paper towels to drain.

Put the oatmeal and the water into a medium pot, and set it over high heat. Bring the water to a boil; then reduce the heat and simmer, stirring occasionally, until the oats are tender, about 20 minutes. Allow to stand for about 10 minutes.

In a small bowl, whisk together the maple syrup and the sambal.

Serve the oatmeal drizzled with the sambal maple syrup and topped with a dollop of the jam, crumbled bacon, and pistachios.

IF USING ROLLED OATS:
COOK'S NOTE
Put 1 ½ cups of oats, 2 ½ cups of water, and ¼ teaspoon of salt into a pot. Bring the water to a boil; then reduce the heat and simmer, uncovered, for about 5 minutes, stirring occasionally. Remove the pot from the heat and let the oatmeal stand for 2 minutes before serving.

Blue Fruit Farm
Winona, Minnesota

An early proponent of the local and organic food movement, **Jim Riddle** is a quiet force of reason when it comes to issues regarding our food, health, and the environment. He's an organic farmer, inspector, educator, policy analyst, and author. Jim's list of accomplishments is long. He was the founding chair of the Winona Farmers Market and the International Organic Inspectors Association, coauthored the International Organic Inspection Manual, served on the Minnesota Department of Agriculture's Organic Advisory Task Force, and was instrumental in crafting the National Organic Standards. With his wife, **Joyce Ford**, he owns and operates Blue Fruit Farm, which provides Birchwood with blueberries, black currants, elderberries, aronia berries, and more. As former chair of the USDA National Organic Standards Board, Jim is a leading voice for organic agriculture and mandatory GMO labeling. We are both active board members of the Right to Know Minnesota Campaign (RTK-MN), a grassroots effort to label genetically engineered foods.

Squash Parsnip Tofu Scramble

(V) GF Serves 4

This light, satisfying brunch dish is easy to make ahead. Earthy roots give the scramble a sweet touch and lots of body.

1 (14-ounce) block firm tofu,
  drained
½ cup plus 1 tablespoon rice bran oil
½ cup fresh orange juice
¼ cup chopped parsley
Salt and freshly ground black pepper
1 onion, diced

1 medium parsnip, diced
½ pound winter squash, diced
  (1 cup)
2 cloves garlic, chopped
1 teaspoon chopped fresh sage
Pinch of red pepper flakes

Slice the block of tofu into inch-thick slabs, and place them between clean dish towels. To remove as much water as possible from the tofu, place a baking sheet over the tofu and weight it. After the tofu has dried for at least 20 minutes (longer if possible), dice it into 1-inch cubes.

Meanwhile, prepare the marinade. Whisk together the ½ cup of oil, orange juice, parsley, a pinch of salt, and some freshly ground black pepper in a large bowl. Submerge the cubed tofu in the marinade for at least 6 hours, or overnight. Strain the tofu, preserving the marinade for another use, if desired.

In a large skillet, heat the remaining tablespoon of oil over medium-low and sauté the onion, parsnip, squash, garlic, and sage for about 2 to 3 minutes. Cover the pan, and cook until the vegetables are soft, about 7 to 9 minutes, adding a drop or two of cold water if the vegetables stick. Add the tofu, and cook for about 10 minutes, stirring often. Season to taste with salt, pepper, and red pepper.

Chili Bean Chili! (V) GF Serves 6 to 8

Boldly seasoned vegan chili is a Birchwood classic. It's chock-full of chickpeas and black beans, and the spiciness is mellowed by a touch of dark cocoa. Double the recipe, make a big potful, and let it simmer away. The chili is terrific with a wedge of Tarragon Cornbread (page 131), and leftovers are great rolled into a tortilla or scooped up with chips.

2 cups black beans, sorted and soaked overnight

1 cup chickpeas, sorted and soaked overnight

3 tablespoons rice bran oil

2 ½ pounds onions, diced

6 cloves garlic, chopped

2 teaspoons salt

1 tablespoon cumin (see note)

1 tablespoon dried oregano

2 tablespoons paprika

1 tablespoon unsweetened cocoa powder

3 tablespoons chili powder, or more to taste

1 to 2 teaspoons chipotle powder, or 2 teaspoons chipotle puree (page 139)

3 cups chopped canned tomatoes, with their juices

2 teaspoons brown sugar

2 tablespoons lime juice, or more to taste

Salt and freshly ground black pepper

½ cup chopped cilantro

FOR MORE ROBUST CUMIN FLAVOR: Roast cumin seeds in a dry skillet until they become fragrant, about 5 seconds. Grind before using.

Drain the beans, and put them in a soup pot with enough fresh water to cover by 4 inches. Set the pot over high heat, and boil for 8 to 10 minutes, skimming off any foam that arises. Lower the heat and simmer, partially covered, until tender, about 60 to 75 minutes.

In a large, heavy pot, heat the oil over medium and sauté the onions until they are tender and beginning to brown, about 7 minutes. Add the garlic, salt, cumin, oregano, paprika, cocoa powder, chili powder, and chipotle. Lower the heat, and cook until the garlic is tender, about 2 or 3 minutes. Add the tomatoes and their juices, brown sugar, lime juice, salt and pepper, and about half (¼ cup) of the cilantro.

Drain the beans when they are soft, reserving the cooking liquid. Add the beans to the tomatoes, adding bean stock if necessary. Simmer another 15 minutes to marry the flavors. Serve garnished with the remaining cilantro.

Spicy Tofu and Quinoa Salad

(V) GF Serves 4 to 6

This hearty salad makes a fine entrée or a nice accompaniment to a bowl of soup. We like to use both red and black quinoa for color and variety; both hold their color when cooked.

1 (14-ounce) block firm tofu, drained

1 tablespoon sesame oil

3 tablespoons sambal

2 tablespoons lime juice

1 cup red or black quinoa, or a mixture

1 cup white quinoa

1 small cucumber, peeled, seeded, and diced

1 small carrot, diced

1 small red bell pepper, diced

1 tablespoon minced jalapeño

1 cup chopped cilantro

½ cup rice bran oil

¼ cup lime juice

1 teaspoon Dijon mustard

1 clove garlic, minced

Salt and freshly ground black pepper to taste

Slice the block of tofu into inch-thick slabs, and place them between clean dish towels. To remove as much water as possible from the tofu, place a baking sheet over the tofu and weight it. After the tofu has dried for at least 20 minutes (longer if possible), dice it into 1-inch cubes.

Heat the sesame oil in a medium skillet set over medium heat, add the tofu, and cook until just warmed through, about 5 minutes. Stir in the sambal and the lime juice. Remove the pan from the heat, and set it aside.

Put all of the quinoa in a fine mesh sieve and rinse it under running water until the water runs clear. Bring 6 cups of water to a boil, and then add a pinch of salt and the quinoa. Lower the heat, cover, and simmer until the quinoa is tender, about 12 to 15 minutes. Pour the quinoa into a fine mesh strainer to remove excess water.

Turn the quinoa into a large bowl, and stir in the tofu, cucumber, carrot, red pepper, jalapeno, and half (½ cup) of the cilantro.

In a small bowl, whisk together the rice bran oil, lime juice, mustard, and garlic.

Pour the dressing over the salad, and toss to coat thoroughly. Garnish with the remaining cilantro.

Beet Chèvre Terrine GF Serves 8

This spectacular presentation is far easier to make than it looks. It makes a wow of a starter, looks great on a buffet, and will keep several days in the refrigerator. Use red beets, and save a little beet juice to whip into some chèvre as a garnish. We like to serve this with hummus and garnish it with Roasted Meyer Lemon Oil (page 230) and pistachios.

4 medium red beets, trimmed
1 pound chèvre
1 tablespoon minced thyme

½ teaspoon grated orange zest
2 tablespoons orange juice
Salt and freshly ground black pepper

Preheat the oven to 400 degrees. Pierce the beets in several places with a sharp knife. Place them in a baking dish and roast until tender, about 45 to 50 minutes. Let the beets cool, and then peel them.

Line a loaf pan or a terrine pan with plastic wrap. Using a very sharp knife or a mandolin, slice the beets as thin as possible. Line the bottom of the pan with a layer of overlapping beet slices.

If desired, set a few tablespoons of the chèvre aside for the garnish (see note). In a small saucepan set over low heat, melt the remaining chèvre, and then whisk in the thyme, orange zest, orange juice, and salt and pepper to taste.

Using two large spoons, smooth a very thin layer of the chèvre mixture over the beets in the pan; then place another layer of beets on top. Continue alternating layers of chèvre and beets until all the beets have been used. Cover and refrigerate for at least 2 hours or up to 2 days. To serve, cut the terrine into slices or squares, and garnish them with a dollop of the remaining cheese.

TO MAKE A FESTIVE FINISH FOR THE BEETS, whip a little beet juice from the roasting pan into the softened reserved chèvre. Or, whip in a squeeze of orange juice and a dash of honey.

Chicken Confit GF Serves 4 to 6

Tender and rich, chicken confit is as delicious as but much easier to make than classic duck confit. The subtle flavor and silky texture come from cooking the meat very slowly in fat. Confit will keep several days in the refrigerator and makes a no-fuss main course that can be crisped up in a few minutes. It's great served on a bed of greens as well as on Chicken Confit Mushroom Pizza (page 121).

It never hurts to have extra confit on hand, so feel free to double or triple the recipe.

4 chicken leg quarters

1 tablespoon salt

1 tablespoon ground black pepper

10 cloves garlic, peeled and smashed

4 bay leaves

6 sprigs fresh thyme

2 teaspoons peppercorns

4 cups rice bran oil

Preheat the oven to 300 degrees.

Season the chicken with the salt and pepper, and place it skin-side down in a large skillet set over medium-high heat. Sear until the chicken is golden brown, about 5 minutes per side. Transfer the chicken to a large deep pan, skin-side up. Add the garlic, bay leaves, thyme, and peppercorns, and cover the chicken completely with the oil. Put the chicken into the oven, uncovered, to bake slowly; the oil should be just barely bubbling. Bake until the meat is very tender and easily pierced with a thin-bladed knife, about 2 to 2 ½ hours.

Cool the chicken and oil together; then remove the chicken from the oil. Strain the oil, transfer it to a lidded container, and store it in the refrigerator for another use. The meat may be refrigerated for several days before using.

To use the chicken, remove the meat from the bones and shred it. To reheat the shredded chicken, put 2 tablespoons of the reserved oil into a skillet over medium heat. Add the chicken and cook until the meat is nicely browned, about 15 minutes. Serve hot or at room temperature.

Chicken Confit Mushroom Pizza

Serves 4 to 6

If you happen to have all the components of this dish prepared in advance, the pizza comes together in a flash. Horseradish Mustard Oil adds a great kick.

1 pound mushrooms, cremini or shiitake or both, brushed clean and stems trimmed

3 tablespoons extra-virgin olive oil

½ teaspoon coarse salt

Cornmeal for dusting the pan

Birchwood Pizza and Flatbread Dough (page 147)

2 to 4 tablespoons Horseradish Mustard Oil (page 231)

1 cup Chicken Confit (page 120)

1 cup shredded Parmesan cheese

1 cup arugula, or 1 cup blanched mustard greens or kale

Salt and freshly ground black pepper

Preheat the oven to 425 degrees. Line a heavy baking sheet with parchment paper. In a medium bowl, toss the mushrooms with the olive oil and the course salt. Arrange the mushrooms on the baking sheet so they are not touching. Roast, turning occasionally, until the mushrooms have browned, about 20 to 25 minutes.

Dust a pizza peel or a rimless baking sheet with cornmeal or a little flour. On a lightly floured surface, roll out the dough into a 9- to 10-inch circle. Place the dough on the pizza peel.

Spread the pizza dough with a healthy slather of the Horseradish Mustard Oil. Then scatter the mushrooms and chicken over the dough. Top lightly with shredded cheese. Gently shake the peel back and forth to make sure the crust is not sticking; then transfer the crust to the oven rack. Bake until the chicken is crispy, the cheese is melted, and the crust is nicely browned, about 10 to 15 minutes. Top the hot pizza with the greens, and season it with salt and pepper.

Cranberry Gastrique (V) GF Makes ½ to ¾ cup

This easy condiment brightens chicken confit, roast vegetables, and roast meats. Serve it alongside the Thanksgiving bird, and swirl it into mayonnaise to accent sandwiches piled high with leftovers. Covered, it keeps several weeks in the refrigerator.

2 cups cranberries
½ cup white wine vinegar
½ cup raspberry vinegar
1 cup sugar, or more to taste

Put the cranberries, vinegars, and sugar into a small saucepan, and bring the mixture to a boil. Lower the heat and simmer, stirring occasionally to avoid scorching, until the liquid is reduced by half, about 10 to 12 minutes.

Puree the gastrique in a blender; then strain it through a fine mesh strainer, using a spatula to guide it through.

Parsnip Pear Sandwich (V) Serves 4

Parsnip Walnut Spread and Roasted Pear Puree layered on thick slices of our hearty multigrain bread make a beautiful sandwich. But here's the thing: these two spreads are also wonderful on their own. Nutty, earthy Parsnip Walnut Spread is a great dip; Roasted Pear Puree is a wonderful condiment for roast pork and chicken. Keep them both on hand.

Parsnip Walnut Spread

1 pound parsnips, peeled and sliced
   (2 cups)
1 tablespoon brown sugar
1 tablespoon lemon juice
¼ cup chopped parsley
¼ cup walnuts, toasted for
   10 minutes at 350 degrees
Salt and freshly ground black pepper

Roasted Pear Puree

2 ripe pears, peeled, quartered, and cored	1 tablespoon lemon juice or cider vinegar, or to taste
1 tablespoon rice bran oil	2 teaspoons honey, or to taste
	Salt and freshly ground black pepper

8 slices thick whole wheat bread	1 small head Boston lettuce, separated into leaves

Make the Parsnip Walnut Spread. Put the parsnip slices in a medium pot, and cover them with water by 1 inch. Set the pot over high heat, and bring the water to a boil. Reduce the heat, and simmer until the parsnips are very tender, about 10 minutes.

Transfer the parsnip slices to a blender or a food processor fitted with a steel blade. Add the sugar, lemon juice, parsley, and walnuts. Puree, drizzling in just enough water to make a stiff puree. Season with salt and black pepper.

To make the Roasted Pear Puree, preheat the oven to 350 degrees and line a small baking sheet with parchment paper. Toss the pears with the oil, and place them on the lined baking sheet. Roast the pears for 30 minutes, turn the pears to coat them in their juices, and continue roasting until the pears are very tender, about 25 to 30 minutes longer. Transfer the pears to a blender or a food processor and puree them with the lemon juice and honey. Season to taste with salt and pepper.

To prepare the sandwiches, spread Parsnip Walnut Spread over four slices of bread. Spread Roasted Pear Puree on the second four slices of bread. Lay the lettuce leaves on top of the Parsnip Walnut Spread, and close the sandwiches.

Birchwood Burger with Duxelles

Serves 4

We buy entire cows from Petersons Limousin Beef. We use the tender cuts for grilled steaks, the tougher cuts for braises and roasts, and the offal for the fun stuff on our charcuterie board; the rest is ground up for our burgers. Here's our favorite version of the classic mushroom and Swiss—a salted patty on a thick layer of rich duxelles topped with a slice of Gruyère and snappy Pickled Red Onions, all on a lightly salted pretzel bun.

Duxelles

3 tablespoons unsalted butter

¼ cup minced shallots

2 pounds cremini mushrooms, stems included, cleaned and chopped

Salt and freshly ground black pepper

¼ cup minced parsley

Burger

1 ½ pounds ground chuck or sirloin, preferably 70% to 75% lean

Coarse salt

4 slices Gruyère

3 tablespoons Birchwood Aioli (page 239) or mayonnaise

½ cup Pickled Red Onions (page 226)

Mixed greens for garnish

4 pretzel buns or your favorite buns

To make the duxelles, melt the butter in a large skillet set over medium heat and sauté the shallots and mushrooms, stirring, until they've given up most of their liquid, about 10 minutes. Turn the heat to low and continue cooking, stirring, until most of the liquid has evaporated. Season well with salt and pepper, and stir in the parsley.

Loosely shape the meat into 4 patties about 4 to 5 inches across. Press your thumb into the center of each patty to give it a dimple. Sprinkle the burgers with coarse salt.

Heat a heavy skillet over medium-high heat for 3 to 4 minutes. Cook the burgers about 3 to 5 minutes per side, depending on desired doneness. Lay a slice of cheese on top of each burger about 2 minutes before they're done.

While the burgers cook, slice open the buns and spread the bottom halves with duxelles and then add some greens. When the burgers are ready, set them on top of the greens. Top the burgers with pickled onions.

WHEN SHAPING BURGERS: Handle the meat as little as possible to avoid compressing it. Dimple each patty with your thumb, making a well in the burger. The dimple helps the burger cook evenly and helps you resist the temptation to squish the burger with a spatula and squeeze out the juice. Salt is crucial; season burgers well just before cooking. The beauty of a burger is its seared crust, and the only way to get it is to make sure the flat top or skillet is very, very hot. We prefer searing in a heavy skillet, not on a grill grate.

Chicken Marsala Serves 4

Our version has all the classiness of the veal dish, but is made with chicken instead. Its richness comes from the mushrooms, and just a touch of cream. We serve the chicken over linguini, garnish it with sautéed leeks and chopped parsley, and add a side of Romanesco.

½ cup unbleached all-purpose flour

Salt and freshly ground black pepper

4 (6- to 8- ounce) boneless, skinless chicken breasts

4 tablespoons (½ stick) unsalted butter

1 large shallot, chopped

1 pound mushrooms, preferably a mixture of shiitake and cremini, brushed clean and torn by hand

1 tablespoon chopped sage

1 cup Marsala

1 cup chicken stock

¼ cup heavy cream

1 to 2 tablespoons lemon juice

¼ cup chopped parsley

1 cup sautéed leeks, optional (see note)

Put the flour in a shallow bowl, and season it with salt and pepper. Place the chicken breasts between two sheets of parchment paper or wax paper, and use a rolling pin or a meat pounder to gently pound the meat until it is about ¼ inch thick. Dredge the chicken in the seasoned flour.

Melt 1 tablespoon of the butter in a large skillet set over medium heat. Working in batches and adding more butter if necessary, cook the chicken breasts until they are golden on both sides, about 3 minutes per side. Transfer the cooked chicken to a plate and set it aside.

Using the same pan, melt the remaining butter. Add the shallots, mushrooms, and sage, and stir. Cover the pan, and cook until the mushrooms have released their juices, about 5 minutes. Remove the lid, and continue cooking until the liquid is reduced to a thin film. Stir in the wine and the stock, scraping up all the nubs clinging to the bottom of the pan. Bring the liquid to a boil, and cook until the sauce begins to thicken, about 3 minutes. Reduce the heat, and stir in the cream.

Return the chicken to the pan, and simmer until the meat is cooked through and the sauce is thick, about 5 to 7 minutes. Season with the lemon juice and salt and pepper to taste.

Spoon the chicken over a bed of linguini, and garnish it with parsley and sautéed leeks.

COOK'S NOTE

TO SAUTÉ LEEKS: Split one large leek in half, trim the whiskers, and rinse, cut-end up, under cold running water. Thinly slice the white and pale-green parts. Discard the dark green parts. Melt 1 tablespoon of butter in a small skillet set over medium heat, and sauté the sliced leek, stirring, until it begins to brown, about 5 to 8 minutes.

Lemon Hazelnut Sea Salt Cookies
Makes 2 to 3 dozen cookies

These cookies are buttery and crumbly and just right with chai tea on a chilly afternoon.

¼ pound (1 stick) unsalted butter, at room temperature

¼ cup granulated sugar

½ cup packed brown sugar

1 teaspoon vanilla extract

Zest and juice of 1 small lemon

1 large egg

2 cups unbleached all-purpose flour

2 teaspoons baking powder

Pinch of fine salt

¼ cup chopped toasted hazelnuts (see note)

1 teaspoon coarse sea salt

2 tablespoons sugar

Preheat the oven to 375 degrees. Line two baking sheets with parchment paper or silicone mats or lightly oil them.

In a mixing bowl, cream the butter; then whip in the sugar, brown sugar, vanilla, lemon zest, and lemon juice. Beat in the egg.

In a separate bowl, stir together the flour, baking powder, and a pinch of fine salt.

Beat the dry ingredients into the butter mixture to make a soft dough. Stir in the hazelnuts. Drop rounded scoops of batter onto the prepared baking sheets, and sprinkle them with the coarse sea salt and the sugar. Bake the cookies until the edges are lightly browned, 10 to 12 minutes.

Let the cookies cool on the baking sheets for several minutes before transferring them to a rack to cool completely. Store in a covered container at room temperature for no more than a day.

TO TOAST HAZELNUTS: Preheat the oven to 350 degrees. Put the hazelnuts on a baking sheet, and bake until the skins turn dark brown and begin to crack and flake, about 10 minutes. Put the warm nuts on a clean kitchen towel, gather up the corners, and gently rub the hazelnuts against each other to remove their skins (not all of it will come off).

Sweet Potato Pie with Oatmeal Walnut Crust Serves 8 to 10

This is one of our most loved pies. It's a surefire recipe for a homey favorite that's great with maple whipped cream or a dollop of ice cream. We use local sweet potatoes: they are skinnier than those shipped from the south and packed with sweet flavor and nutrients.

Crust

1 ½ cups graham cracker crumbs

¾ cup rolled oats

¾ cup ground walnuts

⅓ cup sugar

6 ounces (1 ½ sticks) unsalted butter, melted

Filling

1 ¼ pounds sweet potatoes

⅓ cup unsalted butter

½ cup maple syrup

3 eggs

⅔ cup whole milk

2 teaspoons cinnamon

2 teaspoons nutmeg

½ teaspoon allspice

½ teaspoon ginger

½ teaspoon salt

Preheat the oven to 375 degrees. Prick the sweet potatoes all over with a fork and put them in the oven. Roast the sweet potatoes until they are very tender, about 30 to 45 minutes, or longer, depending on their size. Allow them to cool before cutting them in half and scooping out the flesh into a large bowl.

Meanwhile, put all of the crust ingredients in a large bowl, and work them together. Turn the mixture into a deep 9-inch pie tin, and press it with your fingertips to evenly cover the bottom and sides of the tin. Set the crust aside.

In a small skillet, melt the butter over medium-low heat. When it starts to foam, stir and continue cooking until the butter begins to brown, about 2 to 3 minutes. Remove the pan from the heat, and set the brown butter aside.

In a food processor fitted with a steel blade, puree the cooked sweet potatoes with the brown butter, maple syrup, eggs, milk, cinnamon, nutmeg, allspice, ginger, and salt.

Reduce the oven temperature to 350 degrees. Pour the filling into the prepared piecrust, and bake the pie until the filling is just set, about 40 minutes. Allow the pie to cool before serving.

Tarragon Cornbread GF Serves 8 to 10

This cornbread is perfect with chili or a big bowl of soup. Vary the cheese and the herbs to suit the season. Come summer, we add basil and thyme; in late summer (what we call Scorch), it's rosemary; in fall, use sage.

¼ pound (1 stick) unsalted butter

2 cups medium-ground yellow cornmeal

¾ cup gluten-free all-purpose flour

1 tablespoon baking powder

½ teaspoon baking soda

1 teaspoon salt

2 tablespoons brown sugar

2 large eggs

1 cup buttermilk

½ cup sour cream

2 tablespoons honey

1 ½ cups roasted corn kernels (see page 64)

1 tablespoon minced tarragon

Preheat the oven to 425 degrees. Put the butter in a cast-iron skillet or a 9-inch-square baking pan and put the skillet in the oven to melt the butter. Remove the skillet from the oven, and give it a swirl to coat the skillet with butter. Set the pan aside.

In a large bowl, whisk together the cornmeal, flour, baking powder, baking soda, salt, and brown sugar.

In a smaller bowl, whisk together the eggs, buttermilk, sour cream, honey, and the melted butter from the skillet. Stir in the corn kernels and the tarragon.

Return the skillet to the oven to heat for a minute or two before pouring in the batter. Bake the cornbread until the top is golden brown and a thin knife inserted in the center comes out clean, about 25 minutes. Cool the cornbread on a rack for at least 10 minutes before serving. Serve warm or at room temperature.

Ferndale Market
Cannon Falls, Minnesota

When **John Peterson** returned from college to his hometown of Cannon Falls, he thought it strange that he couldn't find his family's turkeys in the local market. The Petersons have always raised their turkeys the old-fashioned way, with plenty of fresh air and room to roam and without antibiotics or hormones. "It amazed me that here, in the turkey capital of the world, the turkeys were all being shipped in from other states," John says. The Peterson farm became one of the first turkey farms in the state to sell turkeys to local sources. John and his wife, Erika, turned their entrepreneurial talents to local food and created the Ferndale Market, named for John's mom and dad, Fern and Dale. The market, located on the farm and open to the public, features just about every category of local and sustainably produced foods: meat, dairy, eggs, pasta, breads, condiments, and, of course, Ferndale Turkeys from the farm.

Photo: Sarah Hoehn

FROST

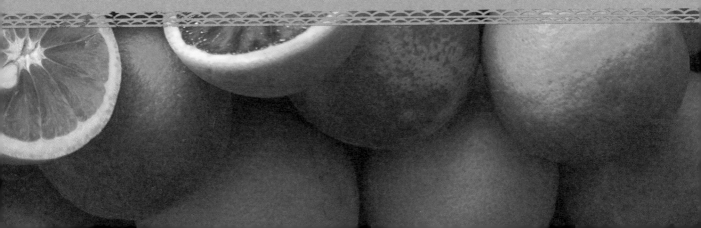

Out in our fields, ghosts of the harvest—stalks and vines, a few errant squash—are coated with silver and glisten in the morning sun. The sudden cold snaps our appetites into action. Hungers surge, and we start roasting roots and cooking whole grains and working with farmstead meats. Now that our shelves are stocked with jars of pickles, fruit butters, jellies, and jams, we are ready to enjoy all the fun of cooking through the cold season. Breakfast is more important than ever this time of year, and we have plenty of bright fresh eggs to make omelets and scrambles laced with farmstead cheese. We love parsnips, Brussels sprouts, carrots, beets—all a little sweeter for their extra time in the fields, kissed with frost. We'll roast them into silky spreads for sandwiches and hearty bases for soups and stews.

Tofu Breakfast Scramble

(V) GF Serves 4 to 6

The marinade can be used again and again. Keep it in a glass container in the refrigerator. Serve the tofu with Kumquat Honey Preserves (page 218).

1 (14-ounce) block firm tofu, drained

½ cup plus 1 tablespoon rice bran oil

½ cup fresh orange juice

¼ cup chopped parsley

Salt and freshly ground black pepper

1 bunch kale, tough ribs removed and leaves torn or chopped (4 cups)

¼ cup diced Pickled Radishes (page 224)

2 tablespoons Roasted Meyer Lemon Oil (page 230)

Green onions

Slice the block of tofu into ½-inch-thick slabs, and place them between clean dish towels. To remove as much water as possible from the tofu, place a baking sheet over the tofu and weight it. After the tofu has dried for at least 20 minutes (longer if possible), dice it into ½-inch cubes.

Meanwhile, prepare the marinade. Whisk together the ½ cup of oil, orange juice, parsley, a pinch of salt, and some pepper in a large bowl.

Submerge the tofu in the marinade for at least 6 hours, or overnight. Strain the tofu, preserving the marinade for another use, if desired.

Preheat the oven to 400 degrees. Line a baking sheet with parchment paper. Place the tofu on the lined baking sheet and roast, turning occasionally, until nicely golden, about 20 to 30 minutes.

Heat the remaining tablespoon of oil in a small skillet set over medium heat, and sauté the kale until it is just limp. Toss in the roasted tofu and radishes, and drizzle with Roasted Meyer Lemon Oil. Serve garnished with green onions.

Buttermilk Sweet Waffles with Cinnamon Whipped Cream Serves 6 to 8

Maple syrup and Cinnamon Whipped Cream puddle in the deep crevices of these light, fluffy waffles. They are fabulous for breakfast and make a terrific afternoon snack.

3 cups unbleached all-purpose flour

1 tablespoon baking powder

¾ teaspoon baking soda

1 teaspoon salt

3 ¼ cups buttermilk

6 ounces (1½ sticks) unsalted butter, melted

3 large eggs, lightly beaten

Rice bran oil or additional butter for the waffle iron

In a large bowl, stir together the flour, baking powder, baking soda, and salt. Mix in the buttermilk, butter, and eggs to make a thick batter.

Preheat the oven to 200 degrees. Heat up the waffle iron and lightly brush the cooking surfaces with oil. When the waffle iron is ready, pour in 1 cup of batter. Cook until the waffle is lightly browned, about 5 to 6 minutes. Transfer the waffle to a baking sheet and keep it warm, uncovered, in the oven until ready to serve. Repeat with the remaining batter.

Serve with a generous dollop of Cinnamon Whipped Cream.

Cinnamon Whipped Cream GF Makes 2 cups

Top off coffee, pound cake, walnut pie, and ice-cream sundaes with this delicious cream. It doesn't keep long, so use it up right away.

1 cup heavy cream

1 to 2 teaspoons ground cinnamon

1 teaspoon vanilla extract

¼ cup fine sugar

Beat the cream until it holds soft peaks; then beat in the cinnamon, vanilla, and sugar. Taste, and adjust the flavors as needed.

Chipotle and Sweet Potato Salad

GF Serves 6 to 8

This spicy, earthy salad is terrific served warm or at room temperature. It works nicely on the buffet table for any type of gathering.

1 ½ pounds sweet potatoes, cut into 1-inch chunks

3 red potatoes, cut into 1-inch chunks

1 tablespoon rice bran oil

1 red onion, diced (1 cup)

2 red bell peppers, seeded and diced

1 bunch green onions, white parts only, sliced

4 cups hearty greens, such as kale, mustard greens, or collards, blanched and sliced

¼ pound bacon, sliced into ½-inch pieces, cooked, and drained

1 teaspoon freshly grated horseradish

½ cup Birchwood Aioli (page 239) or mayonnaise

2 tablespoons chipotle puree (see note)

2 teaspoons lime juice, or more to taste

Salt and freshly ground black pepper

Preheat the oven to 400 degrees. Line a baking sheet with parchment paper. In a medium bowl, toss the sweet potatoes and red potatoes with the oil. Spread them out on the baking sheet, and roast, stirring occasionally, until they are lightly browned and tender, about 20 to 25 minutes. Set aside.

Put the red onion, red peppers, green onions, greens, bacon, and horseradish in a large bowl and toss to combine. Add the cooled sweet potatoes and potatoes.

Whisk together the aioli, chipotle puree, and lime juice.

Pour the dressing over the salad, and toss to coat thoroughly. Season to taste with salt and pepper.

TO MAKE THE CHIPOTLE PUREE: Put two chipotles in a bowl with enough boiling water to just cover the peppers. When the chipotles are plump, about 15 to 20 minutes, drain and seed the peppers. Puree them in a blender or a food processor fitted with a steel blade.

Crystal Ball Farms
Osceola, Wisconsin

Farming is all **Troy DeRosier** wanted to do, and because he grew up on a farm it was all he ever knew. But, just to be sure, he went out on his own and worked another job. It wasn't long before he was back, and soon Troy and his wife, **Barbara**, established Crystal Ball Farms in Osceola, a small village on the banks of the St. Croix River, not far from the Twin Cities. Troy's family had never used farm chemicals, so even before he began he knew he would farm organically. Crystal Ball Farms processes milk from its own herd of one hundred grass-fed Holstein cows and makes butter, cheese, and cheese curds— so tasty with Marshall's ketchup! Their "cream line milk" that we use in the cafe has been pasteurized but not homogenized, and we love that the whole milk comes with that glorious cap of cream on top. "We control everything from growing the crops to the finished milk and cream," Troy says. "That way we know it's the best." The DeRosiers recently installed a 144-kilowatt solar system that supplies 100 percent of the electricity for their farm.

Coconut, Turkey, and Lime Wild Rice Soup GF Serves 4 to 6

Turkey and wild rice soup, a Minnesota standby, gets a bright spin with the addition of coconut and lime. It makes great use of leftover turkey or chicken. Feel free to vary the veggies, but be sure to use fresh limes for snap.

2 tablespoons rice bran oil

1 small onion, chopped

1 carrot, diced

1 stalk celery, diced

1 small red bell pepper, seeded and diced

1 cup cauliflower florets

1 cup cooked wild rice (page 164)

4 to 6 cups chicken or turkey stock

½ cup coconut milk

3 cups diced cooked turkey or chicken

½ cup unsweetened shredded coconut

1 to 2 tablespoons sambal

2 tablespoons lime juice

Salt and freshly ground black pepper

Chopped cilantro

In a large heavy pot, heat the oil over medium and sauté the onion, carrots, celery, red pepper, and cauliflower until they are soft and begin to brown. Stir in the wild rice, stock, coconut milk, turkey, and coconut and bring the soup to a boil. Reduce the heat and simmer for 5 minutes; then stir in sambal to taste, along with the lime juice. Season with salt and pepper to taste. Serve garnished with chopped cilantro.

Birchwood Broccoli Salad

(V) GF Serves 6 to 8

This Birchwood classic is one of the easiest salads to make at home. We like to use the whole head of broccoli; there's plenty of flavor and nutrients in the stem, so no need to throw it away. It's best if the salad has a chance to sit in the refrigerator overnight to allow the flavors to marry.

1 head broccoli, broken into small florets, stems peeled and chopped

¼ cup finely chopped red onion

1 cup dried cranberries

1 cup roasted peanuts or sunflower seeds

1 cup Birchwood Aioli (page 239) or mayonnaise

½ teaspoon cumin

½ teaspoon coriander

Salt and freshly ground black pepper

Put the broccoli, onion, dried cranberries, and peanuts in a medium bowl. In a separate bowl, whisk together the aioli, cumin, and coriander, and season to taste with salt and pepper. Toss the salad with enough dressing to generously coat the broccoli. Cover and refrigerate for at least one hour before serving or, if time allows, overnight.

Maple Ham Pizza Serves 6

We served a variation of this pizza the night Barack Obama won in 2008, adding fresh pineapple in a nod to his Hawaiian roots. No matter your political leanings, it's a winning combination of salty ham and piney rosemary, with a touch of sweet maple.

Cornmeal for the pan

Birchwood Pizza and Flatbread Dough (page 147)

2 tablespoons extra-virgin olive oil

2 shallots, thinly sliced and rings separated

1 tablespoon rosemary leaves, chopped

Salt and freshly ground black pepper

½ pound ham, sliced into thin strips

1 tablespoon maple syrup

½ cup shredded cheddar or other sharp cheese

Preheat the oven to 425 degrees. Dust a pizza peel or a rimless baking sheet with cornmeal. On a lightly floured surface, roll out the dough into a 9- to 10-inch circle and place it on the peel.

Brush the dough with 1 tablespoon of the oil. Gently shake the peel back and forth to make sure the crust is not sticking; then transfer the crust to the oven rack.

Bake the crust until it's puffed and golden, about 5 minutes. Set the crust aside, and leave the oven on.

In a medium bowl, toss together the shallots, rosemary, and remaining tablespoon of oil with a little salt and pepper.

Top the partially cooked crust with the ham, lightly brush on the maple syrup, and then distribute the shallot mixture and the cheese. Bake until the crust is crisp and the ham is nicely browned, about 12 to 15 minutes.

Birchwood Pizza and
Flatbread Dough (V) Makes one 9- to 10-inch crust

There is truly no definitive difference between flatbread and pizza (though some flatbreads do not use yeast). Here's our version. Roll it out as thin as you please for flatbread and a little thicker for pizza, depending on your preference.

At the Birchwood, we also serve a gluten-free pizza using a recipe created by Zoë François, an award-winning, Minneapolis-based pastry chef. Other wonderful gluten-free recipes are featured in the book she wrote with Jeff Hertzberg, *Gluten-Free Artisan Bread in Five Minutes a Day*.

2 teaspoons active dry yeast
½ teaspoon sugar
1 cup warm water

2 to 3 cups high-gluten flour, plus more for kneading dough
2 teaspoons granulated sea salt
Oil for bowl

In a large bowl, combine the yeast, sugar, water, and about ¼ cup of the flour. When the surface begins to foam, gradually work in the remaining flour and the salt. Add just enough flour to make a shaggy dough.

Coat a bowl with oil, and turn the dough into the bowl. Cover the bowl with a dish towel, and place it in a warm spot. Let the dough rise until it has doubled in size, about 1 hour.

Punch the dough down, and turn it onto a lightly floured counter. Knead the dough, adding flour as needed to keep it from sticking.

continued on page 148

continued from page 147

For pizzas, preheat the oven to 425 degrees. Dust a pizza peel or a rimless baking sheet with cornmeal. On a lightly floured surface, roll out the dough into a 9- to 10-inch circle and place it on the peel. Top the pizza according to the directions in the pizza recipe, or create your own pizza recipe. Gently shake the peel back and forth to make sure the crust is not sticking; then transfer the crust to the oven rack. Bake the pizza until the dough is nicely browned and the ingredients are hot, usually 10 minutes or longer, depending on what the pizza is topped with.

For flatbreads, preheat a grill, stovetop pan, or griddle to medium-high. Do not oil the surface. Cut the dough into 4 to 6 pieces. On a lightly floured surface, roll out each piece of dough into a 3- to 4-inch round. Place each flatbread on the grill and let it cook without touching it until you see bubbles on the surface, about 1 to 2 minutes. Turn the flatbread and continue cooking it another 1 to 2 minutes, or until the bread has puffed up.

Turkey Burgers with Creamed Kale GF Serves 4

Our turkey burgers are especially moist and flavorful because we use ground meat from the dark portion of the turkey and mix in sautéed shallot, celery, and garlic. The burgers are topped with lush creamy kale for a sandwich you'll need to eat with both hands. We often feature this on our birdseed bun. Add a fried egg to take it over the top!

1 tablespoon extra-virgin olive oil
2 cloves garlic, chopped
1 large shallot, chopped
1 stalk celery, leaves included, chopped

1 ⅓ pounds ground turkey
1 teaspoon ground pepper
1 teaspoon salt
Rice bran oil for frying the burgers
4 of your favorite buns

Heat the olive oil in a small skillet set over medium heat. Add the garlic, shallot, and celery, and sauté until soft, about 2 minutes.

Put the ground turkey in a medium bowl, and work in the sautéed vegetables and the salt and pepper. Portion out 4 burgers and form them into patties. With your thumb, press a dimple into the middle of each patty.

Heat a large skillet or griddle, and brush it with rice bran oil. Fry the burgers until they are thoroughly cooked through, about 5 minutes per side. The meat should register 165 degrees on a meat thermometer. Serve the burgers on buns piled with creamed kale.

Creamed Kale GF Serves 4

Creamed kale adds flavor, color, and a lush, creamy texture to our turkey burgers. It's great as a side dish, too.

2 pounds kale, tough center ribs removed

4 tablespoons (½ stick) unsalted butter

1 cup heavy cream

⅛ teaspoon freshly grated nutmeg

Salt and freshly ground black pepper

In a pot of boiling, heavily salted water, blanch the kale just until tender, about 30 seconds; then shock it in a bowl of ice water. Drain the kale in a colander, pressing to remove all of the water. Cut the kale into ½-inch ribbons.

Melt the butter in a large sauté pan set over medium heat. Add the kale, cream, and nutmeg. Reduce the heat to low, and cook the kale, stirring often, until the cream has reduced and thickened. Season with salt and pepper to taste.

Sweet Potato Cakes (V) GF Serves 4 to 6

Sweet potato cakes make a great starter, a delicious companion to soup, and a fine vegetarian entrée with a green salad or sautéed vegetables. We often serve them with Tomato Fennel Ragout (page 198), Sweet and Spicy Beets (page 155), and a side of broccoli and bean salad or our Birchwood Broccoli Salad (page 144).

1 large sweet potato
½ cup chickpeas, soaked overnight
½ cup brown rice
2 cloves garlic
1 tablespoon lemon juice
¼ cup tahini

2 tablespoons gluten-free all-purpose flour
2 teaspoons ground coriander
1 teaspoon ground cumin
2 carrots, shredded (1 cup)
Salt and freshly ground black pepper

Preheat the oven to 375 degrees. Prick the sweet potato all over with a fork and put it in the oven. Roast until the sweet potato is very tender, about 45 minutes, or longer, depending on its size. Allow it to cool before cutting it in half and scooping out the flesh.

Drain the chickpeas and put them in a pot with enough fresh water to cover by 2 inches. Set the pot over high heat and boil for 8 to 10 minutes, skimming off any foam that arises. Lower the heat and simmer, partially covered, until tender, about 60 minutes.

Put the rice and a pinch of salt in a small pot with 1½ cups of water. Bring the water to a boil over high heat; then reduce to a simmer, cover the pot, and cook for about 40 minutes. Remove from the heat, and set the covered pot aside for 10 minutes. Remove the lid, and fluff the rice with a fork.

Reduce the oven temperature to 350 degrees. Line a baking sheet with parchment paper.

Puree the sweet potato flesh, chickpeas, garlic, lemon juice, and tahini in a food processor fitted with a steel blade. Turn into a large bowl, and stir in the flour, coriander, cumin, carrots, and rice. Season to taste with salt and pepper.

Portion the cakes using an ice-cream scoop or a ¼-cup measuring cup. Using your hand, flatten each cake to about 1-inch thick. Bake on prepared baking sheet until golden and crisp, about 30 minutes. Serve hot.

COOK'S NOTE

WE USED BROWN RICE IN THIS RECIPE TO MAKE IT GLUTEN FREE. At the Birchwood, we often use Kernza (page 84) instead. If you can eat gluten, farro also works beautifully in place of the brown rice.

Indonesian Chicken Stew

GF Serves 6 to 8

This Indonesian classic, opor ayam, is an aromatic dish that tastes even better the next day after the spices have had a chance to mellow. Serve it over white or brown rice.

2 tablespoons rice bran oil

2 ½ pounds boneless, skinless chicken thighs, cut into 1-inch pieces (see note)

1 jalapeño pepper, seeded, veined, and chopped (1 tablespoon)

4 garlic cloves, thinly sliced

1 large onion, chopped

4 inches fresh ginger, peeled and grated, or more to taste

2 stems lemongrass, halved

1 teaspoon cardamom

1 teaspoon cumin

1 teaspoon coriander

1 teaspoon cinnamon

3 cups chicken stock

½ cup coconut milk

6 to 7 leaves kale, tough ribs removed and leaves julienned

2 tablespoons fresh lime juice, or to taste

Salt and freshly ground black pepper

¼ cup chopped cilantro

Heat 1 tablespoon of the oil in a Dutch oven or a large skillet set over medium-high heat, and sauté the chicken until it is nicely browned on all sides. Transfer the chicken to a plate, and set it aside.

Add the remaining oil to the pan, and sauté the jalapeño, garlic, and onion until the onion is translucent, about 5 minutes. Stir in the ginger, lemon grass, cardamom, cumin, coriander, and cinnamon. Stir in the stock and the coconut milk, scraping up all the nubs from the bottom of the pan. Return the chicken to the pan, stirring to coat it with the sauce. Reduce the heat to medium, and simmer, partially covered, until the chicken is very tender, about 30 to 40 minutes.

Add the kale, and simmer an additional 3 to 4 minutes. Season with the lime juice and salt and pepper. Remove the lemon grass before serving. Garnish the stew with cilantro.

COOK'S NOTE

DON'T HESITATE TO SUBSTITUTE LEFTOVER COOKED CHICKEN in this recipe. Simply omit browning the chicken, and reduce the amount of time the stew simmers after adding the stock and coconut milk to about 15 to 20 minutes. Stir in the cooked chicken when the kale goes in, and follow the recipe as written from that point.

Pumpkin Hand Pie Makes 4 hand pies

This recipe for hand pies serves us through the seasons. The fun is deciding what to fill these with and what garnish will work best. The pies freeze nicely. The dough is simple to work with and also freezes well. Make an extra batch of dough to have on hand for future pies.

We garnish these hand pies with Sweet and Spicy Beets (page 155) for color and snap and serve them with parsnip puree and a small green salad.

1 (2 ½- to 3-pound) pumpkin, halved and seeded

1 medium turnip, peeled and cut into small dice

2 tablespoons rice bran oil

½ pound cipollini onions, peeled

2 tablespoons chopped thyme

½ cup white wine

¼ cup maple syrup

½ cup shredded Gruyère

Salt and freshly ground black pepper

Birchwood Hand Pie Dough (page 155)

Preheat the oven to 350 degrees. Line a baking sheet with parchment paper, and put the pumpkin cut-side down on the parchment paper. Roast until very soft, about 1 hour. Allow the pumpkin to cool a little before scooping the flesh into a large bowl and mashing it. Measure out 1 cup of mashed pumpkin for the filling, and save the rest for another use.

Toss the turnips with a little oil and salt, and spread them out on a baking sheet. Roast until the turnips are tender but firm, about 10 minutes.

Toss the onions with a little oil, and roast until the onions are golden and very soft, about 20 minutes. Coarsely chop the roasted onions with a sharp knife.

Stir the roasted turnips, onions, thyme, wine, maple syrup, and cheese into the mashed pumpkin, and season with salt and pepper to taste. Allow the mixture to cool before stuffing the hand pies.

Raise the oven temperature to 375 degrees, and line the baking sheet with fresh parchment paper.

continued on page 155

continued from page 153

Divide the dough into 4 equal balls. Working on a lightly floured surface, use a lightly floured rolling pin to roll each ball of dough into an 8-inch circle. Mound ½ cup of the filling into the center of each one. Bring the edges of the dough together, and press to seal the edges. Bake until the crust is firm and nicely browned, about 20 to 25 minutes.

Birchwood Hand Pie Dough Makes 4 hand pies

This is one of the most forgiving pastry doughs. It comes together in a snap and is great for hand pies and pastries.

¼ pound (1 stick) unsalted butter
¼ pound cream cheese
¼ cup heavy cream

1 ½ cups unbleached all-purpose flour
½ teaspoon salt

Using a stand mixer with a paddle attachment or a hand mixer, whip together the butter, cream cheese, and cream. Add the flour and salt, and stir just until the dough holds together in a ball. Turn the dough out onto a well-floured surface, flatten it into a disk, and wrap it in parchment paper. Refrigerate the dough for at least 30 minutes before using it.

Sweet and Spicy Beets (V) GF Serves 4 to 6

These brilliant magenta beets will keep at least a week in the refrigerator and are wonderful added to salads or as a side to burgers and sandwiches. The sweet, spicy flavors and color perk up Pumpkin Hand Pies (page 153).

2 large beets, trimmed and scrubbed
2 cloves garlic, minced

2 tablespoons honey
1 teaspoon sambal, or more to taste

Preheat the oven to 350 degrees. Place the beets on a baking sheet, and roast them until a thin knife is easily inserted into the center, about 40 to 50 minutes. Allow the beets to cool before peeling them. Cut the peeled beets into ½-inch cubes.

In a large bowl, whisk together the garlic, honey, and sambal. Turn the beets into the bowl, stirring to coat the beets with the dressing. Store, refrigerated, in a covered container.

Grapefruit Bran Muffins Makes 12 muffins

Our hearty, moist, honey-sweet muffins are graced with pepitas, sunflower seeds, and flax seeds and sparked with tangy grapefruit, perfect for wintery breakfasts on the go. We like the flavor and textures of these different seeds, but feel free to choose just one or two, depending on what you have on hand.

1 cup unbleached all-purpose flour
1 teaspoon baking soda
¼ teaspoon salt
1 cup wheat bran (not cereal)
1 tablespoon sunflower seeds
1 tablespoon flax seeds
1 tablespoon pepitas

¼ pound (1 stick) unsalted butter, at room temperature
¼ cup sugar
¼ cup honey
1 large egg
1 cup plain Greek-style yogurt
2 tablespoons grated grapefruit zest
2 tablespoons fresh grapefruit juice

Preheat the oven to 400 degrees. Line the cups of a 12-muffin tin with muffin papers.

In a medium bowl, mix together the flour, baking soda, salt, wheat bran, sunflower seeds, flax seeds, and pepitas.

In a large bowl, beat together the butter, sugar, and honey; then beat in the egg, yogurt, grapefruit zest, and juice. Add the dry ingredients to the wet ingredients, and stir until just combined (the batter will be lumpy). Spoon the batter into the lined muffin cups, filling each about two-thirds full.

Bake until the muffins are golden brown and springy to the touch, about 15 to 20 minutes. Turn the muffins out onto a rack to cool.

Pumpkin Cheesecake GF Serves 10 to 12

Creamy and flavorful, this cheesecake is a classic. We love heirloom
Cinderella pumpkins from Greg Reynolds at Riverbend Farm. Feel free
to substitute butternut squash or sweet potatoes for the pumpkin.

Crust

4 ounces gluten-free gingersnap
cookies (about 20 cookies)

¼ cup walnuts or pecans

2 tablespoons walnut oil or rice bran
oil

Filling

1 pound cream cheese

¾ cup sugar

2 tablespoons gluten-free all-
purpose flour

2 teaspoons vanilla extract

2 large eggs

1 cup pumpkin puree (see note)

1 teaspoon cinnamon

1 teaspoon ginger

¼ teaspoon allspice

Preheat the oven to 325 degrees.

To make the crust, grind the gingersnaps and walnuts in a food
processor fitted with a steel blade. Add the oil, and process to make a
firm dough. Turn the dough into a 9-inch springform pan, and press it
evenly against the bottom and sides of the pan. Bake the crust until it is
just firm, about 5 minutes.

To make the filling, put all of the ingredients in a large bowl and beat
until smooth. Pour the filling into the prepared crust. Bake until the
cheesecake peaks in the center, about 60 to 75 minutes.

Let the cheesecake cool to room temperature before removing the sides
of the pan. Transfer the cheesecake to a serving plate, and cover it
loosely with parchment paper. Chill the cheesecake for at least 2 hours
before slicing it.

IF GREG'S HEIRLOOM
CINDERELLA PUMPKINS
AREN'T AVAILABLE, choose
small, sweet pie or sugar
pumpkins for any of our
pumpkin recipes. Field pumpkins are
tough and stringy; they're grown for
carving jack-o'-lanterns, not cooking.
Roast pumpkin as you would squash:
cut it in half, remove the seeds (and
rinse and roast those), and place the
halves cut-side down on a baking sheet
lined with parchment paper. Roast in a
350-degree oven until very tender, about
1 hour.

Garden Farme
Ramsey, Minnesota

There's no missing **Bruce Bacon**, an elder in our permaculture community. Bruce's gray beard, baggy green work pants, and thick boots suggest his personal history and passion for growing real food. Homesteaded in 1913, Garden Farme is the last registered farm in Ramsey County; Bruce transitioned the land to organic in 1977. Along with raising bees and all manner of produce and notable garlic, Garden Farme is a small agribusiness incubator where young farmers and food producers learn their trades. Bruce is on the forefront of the local food movement, deeply engaged in policy, education, and environmental matters.

WINTER

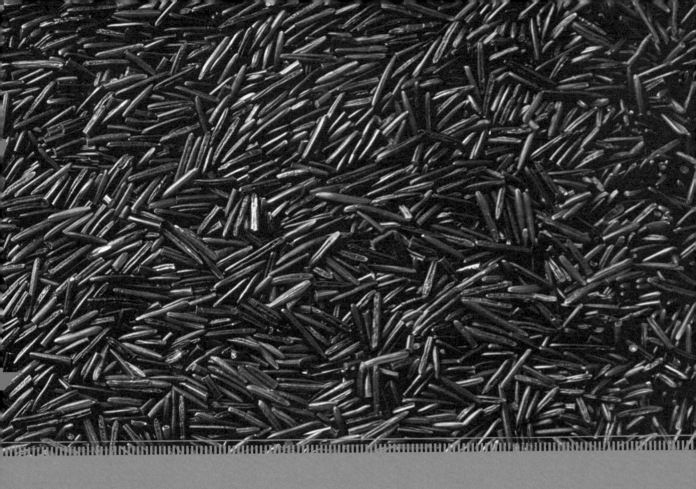

Winter is the season for cooks! Put on a pot of chili or a hearty stew, and the windows glaze with a frosty sheen that mirrors the glow of candles. Now is the time to bake cookies and bars for the holidays, time to lounge by the fire and sip cocoa. Marshall is a maestro of the citrus season: he uses kumquats, grapefruits, Meyer lemons, Cara Caras, blood oranges, satsumas, and all manner of tangerines to brighten wintery foods. And who says you can't eat locally in the winter? Take a look at these recipes calling for hearty roasts, earthy roots, squashes, farm-fresh eggs, and artisan cheeses.

Apple Turnip Quiche Serves 6 to 8

Sweet, tart apple makes a nice foil to turnip's sharper edge in this wintery quiche. Sometimes we use celery root instead of turnip, and rutabaga works nicely as well.

Basic Pastry Crust (page 5)

1 medium apple, peeled, cored, and diced

1 medium turnip, peeled and diced

1 tablespoon rice bran oil

5 large eggs

½ cup heavy cream

1 ½ cups whole milk

¼ teaspoon salt

⅛ teaspoon freshly ground black pepper

2 teaspoons thyme leaves

1 cup shredded Gruyère

Preheat the oven to 425 degrees. Roll out the pastry dough, and fit it into a deep 9-inch pie pan. Line the crust with parchment paper, and weight it with pie weights, dried beans, or rice. Bake the crust for about 12 minutes. Set the crust aside.

In a medium bowl, toss the apples and turnips with the oil, and spread them out on a baking sheet. Roast, shaking the pan occasionally, until the apples are very soft and the turnips begin to brown, about 10 to 15 minutes. Set the apples and turnips aside.

Reduce the oven temperature to 350 degrees. In a large bowl, whisk together the eggs, cream, milk, salt, pepper, and thyme, and stir in half (½ cup) of the cheese. Stir in the apples and turnips. Place the prebaked crust on a baking sheet and carefully pour the filling into the crust. Top with the remaining ½ cup of cheese. Carefully transfer the baking sheet to the oven. Bake the quiche until the filling is just set but still moist, about 40 minutes. The quiche should jiggle a little in the middle. Let the quiche cool on a rack before cutting it. Serve at room temperature.

Smoked Turkey and
Citrus Wild Rice Salad GF Serves 4 to 6

Marshall is a wiz at vinaigrettes, coulis, and snappy condiments
that make familiar dishes fresh and exciting. (Just take a look at the
recipes for vinaigrettes and sauces in the Pantry chapter!) We love how
Orange Honey Vinaigrette perks up the smoked turkey and the nutty
wild rice, but you may find other vinaigrettes you like better or whose
ingredients you have on hand, such as Cranberry Vinaigrette (page 233)
or Horseradish Vinaigrette (page 233). Feel free to mix and match and
make this dish your own.

½ cup wild rice

½ pound torn smoked turkey or
   chicken (1 cup)

1 stalk celery, diced

1 small white onion, diced (½ cup)

1 small red bell pepper, seeded and
   diced

½ cup dried cherries

½ cup Orange Honey Vinaigrette
   (page 234)

Salt and freshly ground black pepper

2 small oranges or satsumas, peeled
   and sectioned

5 to 6 ounces mixed greens

Microgreens

To cook the wild rice, bring 3 cups of water to a boil. Add the wild rice
and a pinch of salt, and reduce the heat. Simmer the rice until it is
tender, about 40 minutes. Drain the rice, and let it cool.

Put the wild rice, chicken, celery, onions, bell pepper, and cherries into a
large bowl, and toss with just enough vinaigrette to lightly coat. Season
the salad with salt and pepper.

Arrange the mixed greens on a large platter or individual serving plates.
Spoon the salad onto the mixed greens. Garnish the salad with orange
slices and microgreens.

Blue Cheese, Walnut, Roasted Pear Puree, and Pickled Onion Pizza Serves 4 to 6

This simple pizza is easy to assemble. The Roasted Pear Puree is also a wonderful condiment for roast pork or chicken. It keeps about a week, covered, in the refrigerator.

Blue Cheese Walnut Spread

½ cup crumbled blue cheese

⅓ cup walnuts, toasted at 350 degrees for 10 minutes

¼ cup sour cream

2 ounces cream cheese

2 tablespoons heavy cream or half-and-half

Salt and freshly ground black pepper

Roasted Pear Puree

2 ripe pears, peeled, quartered, and cored

1 tablespoon rice bran oil

1 tablespoon lemon juice or cider vinegar, or to taste

2 teaspoons honey, or to taste

Salt and freshly ground black pepper

Cornmeal for the pan

Birchwood Pizza and Flatbread Dough (page 147)

1 cup thinly sliced hearty greens, such as kale or mustard greens

Pickled Red Onions (page 226)

To make the Blue Cheese Walnut Spread, put the blue cheese, walnuts, sour cream, cream cheese, and cream into a food processor fitted with a steel blade. Process, adding more cream as needed. Season the spread with salt and pepper, and set it aside.

continued on page 166

continued from page 165

To make the Roasted Pear Puree, preheat the oven to 350 degrees and line a small baking sheet with parchment paper. Toss the pears with the oil, and place them on the lined baking sheet. Roast the pears for 30 minutes, turn the pears to coat them in their juices, and continue roasting until the pears are very tender, about 25 to 30 minutes longer. Transfer the pears to a blender or a food processor and puree them with the lemon juice and honey. Season to taste with salt and pepper.

Raise the oven temperature to 425 degrees. Dust a pizza peel or a rimless baking sheet with cornmeal. On a lightly floured surface, roll out the dough into a 9- to 10-inch circle and place it on the pizza peel. Gently shake the peel back and forth to make sure the crust is not sticking; then transfer the crust to the oven rack. Bake the crust until it is firm and crusty brown, about 5 to 10 minutes.

Spread the blue cheese mixture over the warm crust; then smooth on some Roasted Pear Puree. Arrange the greens over the pear puree, and top the pizza with pickled onions.

French Fries! (V) GF Serves 4

Serve with lots of Birchwood Ketchup (page 241).

2 ½ pounds russet potatoes, scrubbed and cut into ¼-inch sticks

6 cups rice bran oil
Salt and freshly ground black pepper

Pour the oil into a deep saucepan, and heat it to 325 degrees. Working in small batches, drop the fries into the oil, and cook them for about 10 minutes. Remove the fries from the oil with a slotted spoon or a spider, and set them aside.

Increase the oil temperature to 375 degrees. Working in small batches, return the fries to the oil, and fry them until they are golden and crispy. Use a slotted spoon or a spider to transfer the fries to a thick paper bag or paper towels. Allow the oil to heat back up to 375 degrees between batches. Season and serve immediately.

Winter Vegetable Hand Pie Serves 4

Roasted roots and robust Parmesan are wrapped in a firm, flaky crust, set on creamy Sunchoke Puree, and topped with Pear Cranberry Chutney (page 217) and a drizzle of Blood Orange Gastrique (page 169).

Birchwood Hand Pie Dough
  (page 155)
1 medium turnip, peeled and diced
2 medium parsnips, peeled and diced
1 medium beets, peeled and diced
1 tablespoon rice bran oil
6 leaves kale, tough center ribs removed and leaves cut into ½-inch strips

2 tablespoons white wine or lemon juice
½ cup grated Parmesan cheese
2 tablespoons maple syrup
Salt and freshly ground black pepper
Sunchoke Puree (recipe follows)
Pear Cranberry Chutney (page 217)
Blood Orange Gastrique (page 169)

Preheat the oven to 375 degrees. Line a baking sheet with parchment paper.

In a large bowl, toss the turnips, parsnips, and beets with the oil. Spread the vegetables on the baking sheet so none of the vegetables touch. Roast the vegetables, stirring occasionally, until they are nicely browned on all sides, about 20 minutes.

Scrape the vegetables into a bowl. Toss in the kale, wine, cheese, and maple syrup. Season to taste with salt and pepper.

Line the baking sheet with fresh parchment paper.

Divide the dough into 4 equal balls. Working on a lightly floured surface, use a lightly floured rolling pin to roll each ball of dough into an 8-inch circle. Mound ½ cup of the filling into the center of each one. Bring the edges of the dough together, and press to seal the edges. Bake until the crust is firm and nicely browned, about 20 to 25 minutes.

Serve warm on a bed of Sunchoke Puree. Top the hand pies with Pear Cranberry Chutney and Blood Orange Gastrique.

Sunchoke Puree GF

This puree makes a fine pillow for Winter Vegetable Hand Pies and Pumpkin Hand Pies (page 153), and it's lovely with beef brisket or roast chicken.

1 pound sunchokes, scrubbed and cut into 2-inch pieces
3 tablespoons unsalted butter, at room temperature

1 cup heavy cream
¼ cup orange juice
Salt and freshly ground black pepper

Put the sunchokes and a pinch of salt into a medium saucepan and add just enough water to cover them. Bring the water to a boil; then reduce the heat. Simmer, uncovered, until the sunchokes are very tender, about 20 to 30 minutes. Drain.

Mash the sunchokes with the butter, cream, and orange juice. Season to taste with salt and pepper.

Blood Orange Gastrique Makes 1 cup

This simple sauce is delicious drizzled over roasted root vegetables and on roast chicken or pork. It will keep for a week, covered, in the refrigerator.

1 cup sugar
¼ cup white balsamic vinegar
¼ cup cider vinegar

Juice of 6 medium blood oranges
1 tablespoon grated blood orange zest

Put the sugar, vinegars, juice, and zest into a small heavy saucepan and bring it to a boil. Reduce the heat to medium, and simmer until the liquid is reduced by half and is thickened, about 5 to 8 minutes.

Pour the sauce into a nonreactive bowl. Allow the gastrique to cool before transferring it to a glass container to store.

Whole Grain Milling
Welcome, Minnesota

Whole Grain Milling is one of the region's largest organic mills, processing every kind of local grain, including wheat, rye, and oats, as well as packaging dried beans from organic growers in the region. "My father tried to use chemicals early on, back in the 1940s, but things just didn't feel right to him," says **Doug Hilgendorf**, who now farms and runs the mill along with his family. "The birds went away, and it became far too quiet. So Dad returned to his traditional ways of farming, and I have followed in his footsteps by farming organically."

We feature Whole Grain Milling Tortilla Chips as a side to our sandwiches and for dipping. Made with high-lysine corn, they are full of protein and loaded with real corn flavor. Mixing the golden chips with the blue is a pretty combination.

Winter Veggie and Tofu Sauté with Gingered Garlic Sauce

(V) GF Serves 4 to 6

Keep this Gingered Garlic Sauce on hand to finish a simple stir-fry and gussy up a casual sauté. It gives roasted squash and sweet potatoes a lift. Vary the vegetables using what looks good at the market and what you have on hand. Serve the sauté over brown rice, quinoa, or farro.

Tofu

2 inches ginger, grated (2 tablespoons)	1 tablespoon tamari
	3 tablespoons dark sesame oil
2 cloves garlic, minced	1 (14-ounce) block firm tofu

Gingered Garlic Sauce

2 inches ginger, grated (2 tablespoons)	3 tablespoons dark sesame oil
	1 tablespoon tamari
2 cloves garlic, minced	

Veggies

2 tablespoons sesame oil	1 small red onion, diced
1 medium turnip, peeled and cut into matchsticks	½ cup Brussels sprouts, trimmed and quartered
2 carrots, cut into matchsticks	½ cup rapini (broccoli raab), cut into ¼-inch pieces

Slice the block of tofu into inch-thick slabs, and place them between clean dish towels. To remove as much water as possible from the tofu, place a baking sheet over the tofu and weight it. After the tofu has dried for at least 20 minutes (longer if possible), dice it into 1-inch cubes.

Meanwhile, prepare the marinade. Whisk together the ginger, garlic, tamari, and sesame oil in a large bowl. Submerge the tofu cubes in the marinade for at least 6 hours, or overnight. Drain the tofu, and pat it dry.

Make the Gingered Garlic Sauce. Put all of the sauce ingredients into a jar with a lid. Cover tightly, and shake.

Film a large skillet or a wok with the sesame oil, and set it over medium-high heat. Toss in the vegetables, and sauté until they begin to soften, about 2 minutes. Toss in the tofu, cover the skillet, and continue cooking until the vegetables are heated through, about 3 to 5 minutes. Stir in just enough of the Gingered Garlic Sauce to lightly coat the sauté, and serve over brown rice.

Mushroom Mac and Cheese

Serves 4 to 6

If you can get your hands on wild mushrooms—any wild mushrooms—please include them in this dish. This rich, creamy mac and cheese is a winning alternative to the classic weeknight dish, simple yet elegant and a fine meal for a casual dinner with friends. The white cheddar sauce is sharp enough to give this comfort food a lot of character. At the Birchwood, we garnish the mac and cheese with toasted bread crumbs and serve it with blanched or sautéed vegetables such as radish, turnips, or Romanesco.

White Cheddar Sauce

4 tablespoons (½ stick) unsalted butter

1 clove garlic, minced

¼ cup unbleached all-purpose flour

1 quart whole milk

½ cup white wine

1 pound sharp cheddar cheese, grated

1 teaspoon freshly grated black pepper

½ teaspoon grated nutmeg

continued on page 175

continued from page 173

Mushrooms

2 tablespoons unsalted butter

½ pound shiitake mushrooms, stemmed and sliced

1 pound pasta (rotini and linguine work well)

Salt

½ pound cremini mushrooms, stemmed and sliced

¼ cup dry sherry

½ cup toasted bread crumbs (see note)

¼ cup chopped parsley

COOK'S NOTE

TO TOAST BREAD CRUMBS: Put several slices of day-old bread into a food processor fitted with a steel blade, and process the bread into crumbs. Spread the bread crumbs on a baking sheet, and toast them in a 350-degree oven until they are lightly browned, about 5 to 8 minutes.

Make the sauce. Melt the butter in a large, heavy saucepan over medium-low heat. Add the garlic and cook about 30 seconds; then whisk in the flour. Continue cooking, stirring, until the flour forms a paste, about 1 to 2 minutes. Slowly whisk in the milk. Simmer until the sauce becomes thick, about 2 more minutes. Whisk in the white wine, and then slowly stir in the cheese, pepper, and nutmeg.

For the mushrooms, melt the butter in a medium skillet over medium heat. Add the mushrooms and cook until they are tender, about 5 to 7 minutes. Add the sherry and sauté until it's absorbed, another minute or two. Turn the mushrooms into the sauce.

Bring a large pot of water to a rolling boil, and add a little salt. Cook the pasta until it is al dente, about 6 to 8 minutes. Drain.

To complete the dish, fold the cooked pasta into the sauce. Serve garnished with toasted bread crumbs and chopped parsley.

Brandied Turkey Stew with Cauliflower Sweet Potato Puree

GF Serves 6 to 8

This rich, satisfying stew is just right for a midwinter gathering.
Make it ahead early in the day, then relax or go out for a ski. The stew
practically cooks itself. Serve it over Cauliflower Sweet Potato Puree,
mashed potatoes, or rice and add a spoonful of Cranberry Quince
Chutney (page 218).

1 (3 ½ pound) turkey breast	¼ cup gluten-free all-purpose flour
1 cup heavy cream	2 cups chicken stock
½ cup white wine	½ cup brandy
2 medium parsnips, diced	1 tablespoon chopped tarragon
3 medium carrots, diced	1 tablespoon chopped rosemary
6 red potatoes, diced	Pinch of ground juniper berries
1 large onion, diced	Salt and freshly ground black pepper
2 tablespoons unsalted butter	1 cup frozen peas, thawed

Preheat the oven to 350 degrees. Place the turkey, cream, and wine into
a Dutch oven. If the liquid doesn't cover the turkey, add just enough
water to cover. Slowly poach the turkey breast until it is tender and the
juices run clear when poked with a knife, about 60 to 90 minutes. A meat
thermometer inserted into the turkey breast should read 160 degrees.
Remove the turkey from the pot, and reserve the poaching liquid. Allow
the turkey to cool a little before chopping it into 1-inch chunks. Set it
aside.

Put the parsnips, carrots, and potatoes in a stockpot, and add enough
water to cover by 1 inch. Set the pot over high heat. Bring the water to
a boil; then lower the heat. Simmer the vegetables until they are just
tender, about 10 to 15 minutes, and then drain them.

AT THE BIRCHWOOD, WE
SQUEEZE THE MOST OUT OF
EVERY INGREDIENT: nothing
goes to waste. Scraps from
diced turnips go into a soup
rather than the compost pile. Leftover
fresh leeks from one menu will become a
pickled leek garnish for the next. We try
to keep our waste to the very minimum by
finding creative ways to use up the odds
and ends.

continued on page 178

continued from page 176

To make the sauce, melt the butter in a large pot over medium heat, and sauté the onions until they are translucent, about 5 minutes. Whisk in the flour and cook to make a thick paste, about 1 to 2 minutes. Whisk in ½ cup of the reserved poaching liquid and the chicken stock, brandy, tarragon, rosemary, and juniper. Cook until the sauce has thickened and the flavors have blended, about 3 to 5 minutes.

Add the turkey and the vegetables to the sauce and mix gently. Add salt and pepper to taste. Stir in the peas. Serve the stew on a bed of Cauliflower Sweet Potato Puree.

Cauliflower Sweet Potato Puree GF Serves 6

This puree is a flavorful bed for any stew and makes a fine side dish for roast chicken or sautéed pork chops.

1 small head cauliflower, quartered, stemmed, and broken into florets (2 cups)

1 medium sweet potato, diced (1 cup)

2 small turnips, peeled and diced (1 cup)

1 cup vegetable stock

2 tablespoons unsalted butter, at room temperature

½ cup heavy cream

½ cup shredded provolone cheese

Salt and freshly ground black pepper

Put the cauliflower, sweet potatoes, turnips, and stock into a medium saucepan. Set the pan over high heat, and bring the stock to a boil. Reduce the heat, cover, and simmer until the vegetables are very soft, about 5 to 10 minutes. Remove the lid, and continue cooking until the stock has evaporated.

Turn the vegetables into a food processor fitted with a steel blade and puree, adding the butter and cream. Pulse in the cheese, and season to taste with salt and pepper.

Hidden Stream Farm
Elgin, Minnesota

Not far from the Mississippi River Bluffs in southern Minnesota, the Klein family raises animals on a grass-based system to make them healthy and strong. The pigs enjoy a Swedish "deep-bedded environment," a hoop structure that provides shade and cooling breezes in summer and allows them to snuggle into deep insulating straw bedding to stay warm come wintertime. The Kleins also raise feed—corn, barley, and hay—on the farm's rolling green hills. **Lisa and Eric Klein** both grew up in farm families, and they are graduates and now mentors of the Land Stewardship Project Farm Beginnings program, which helps young farmers get growing. Each week, Lisa attends a produce auction in southern Minnesota to scout out organic fruits and veggies from neighboring farms. With our weekly pork delivery, she will also send strawberries, black raspberries, pears, sweet corn, and other seasonal goodies.

Photos: Becca Dilley

Tangelo Thyme Mini Donuts

(V) GF Makes about 18 donuts

These donuts are such a hit that one of our customers requested them for the special dessert at her wedding. Delicate and light, they fly out of the case each morning. When tangelos are not available, feel free to substitute tangerines, oranges, or Meyer lemons.

Donuts

2 cups sugar

1 ½ cups brown rice flour

⅔ cup garbanzo bean flour

1 ½ cups potato starch flour

½ cup arrowroot starch flour

1 tablespoon baking powder

1 teaspoon xanthan gum

1 teaspoon salt

½ teaspoon baking soda

⅔ cup sunflower oil

⅔ cup applesauce

2 tablespoons vanilla extract

1 ½ cups hot water, not boiling

Grated zest from 2 tangelo oranges, 1 to 2 teaspoons reserved

2 tablespoons chopped thyme, or 2 teaspoons dried

Glaze

Juice from 2 tangelo oranges

2 cups powdered sugar

Reserved grated zest

Granulated sugar

Preheat the oven to 350 degrees. Lightly grease a donut pan with sunflower oil.

In a large bowl, stir together the sugar, brown rice flour, garbanzo bean flour, potato starch flour, arrowroot starch flour, baking powder, xanthan gum, salt, and baking soda.

continued on page 182

continued from page 181

In a separate bowl, whisk together the sunflower oil, applesauce, vanilla, hot water, zest (except the amount reserved for the glaze), and thyme.

Stir the wet ingredients into the dry ingredients. Spoon the batter into the prepared donut pan. Bake until the donuts are light golden and solid to the touch, about 20 minutes.

While the donuts are baking, make the glaze. In a small bowl, whisk together the tangelo juice and powdered sugar.

When the donuts are cool enough to handle, lightly brush on the glaze and garnish the donuts with a sprinkle of zest and sugar. Allow to cool before serving.

Maple Oatmeal Crème Brûlée

GF Serves 6 to 8

Dessert for breakfast? What a great way to start a bitter winter morning. Crack into the lovely maple glaze on top of this rich, satisfying oatmeal before you crack into the ice outside the door. You can assemble this oatmeal the night before, and it makes a great brunch on a snowy Saturday.

¼ cup maple syrup
¼ teaspoon salt
3 ⅓ cups milk
2 eggs

2 teaspoons vanilla extract
2 ¼ cups rolled oats
2 tablespoons maple sugar or brown sugar
½ teaspoon ground cinnamon

Preheat the oven to 350 degrees. Lightly butter an 8 × 11-inch baking dish or 8 individual custard cups.

Whisk together the maple syrup, salt, milk, eggs, and vanilla. Stir in the oats. Pour the mixture into the prepared baking dish. If using custard cups, place them on a baking sheet. Bake until the center is jiggly but not runny and the edges are slightly brown, about 40 to 45 minutes (20 to 25 minutes for custard cups).

Preheat the broiler. Stir together the sugar and the cinnamon and sprinkle it over the oatmeal. Place the pan under the broiler until the sugar bubbles and browns slightly, about 1 to 2 minutes.

Cream Cheese Pumpkin Brownies

Makes about 40 small brownies

These brownies are more than just brownies: they are a rich, layered, elegant dessert. The brownie base supports a sweetened cream cheese layer, a spiced pumpkin layer, and a dark chocolate ganache.

Brownie Layer

10 ounces bittersweet chocolate, chopped

6 ounces (1 ½ sticks) unsalted butter, cut into pieces

1 ½ cups sugar

2 teaspoons vanilla extract

4 large eggs

1 cup unbleached all-purpose flour

½ teaspoon salt

Cream Cheese Layer

8 ounces cream cheese

6 tablespoons (¾ stick) unsalted butter, at room temperature

1 ½ cups powdered sugar

1 teaspoon vanilla extract

Pumpkin Layer

4 tablespoons (½ stick) unsalted butter, at room temperature

2 cups powdered sugar

¼ cup pumpkin puree

2 teaspoons cinnamon

1 teaspoon ginger

½ teaspoon nutmeg

¼ teaspoon cloves

Ganache

½ pound dark chocolate, chopped

½ cup heavy cream

Preheat the oven to 350 degrees. Butter and flour a 9 × 13-inch baking pan, tapping out the excess flour.

Melt the chocolate and the butter in a medium metal bowl set over barely simmering water, stirring until smooth. Set the bowl aside, and allow the chocolate to cool slightly.

For the brownie layer, whisk the sugar and the vanilla into the chocolate; then whisk in the eggs one at a time to make a smooth batter. Stir in the flour and the salt. Spread the batter evenly in the prepared pan. Bake the brownies until a toothpick inserted into the center comes out clean, about 20 to 25 minutes. Set the pan on a rack until the brownies cool completely, about 1 hour.

For the cream cheese layer, put the cream cheese and the butter in a large bowl, and beat with an electric mixer on medium speed until light and fluffy. Sift in the powdered sugar; then add the vanilla and beat until smooth. Spread the cream cheese mixture evenly over the cooled brownie layer, and refrigerate until firm, about 30 minutes.

For the pumpkin layer, whip the butter, powdered sugar, and pumpkin puree; then whip in the cinnamon, ginger, nutmeg, and cloves. Spread the pumpkin mixture over the cooled cream cheese layer. Return the pan to the refrigerator until the pumpkin layer is firm, about 30 more minutes.

To make the ganache, put the chocolate and the cream in a small, heavy saucepan set over low heat. Heat, stirring, until the chocolate is melted and the ganache is very smooth. Remove the pan from the heat.

Spread a thick layer of ganache over the cooled pumpkin layer. Refrigerate until firm, about 15 minutes. Cut into small squares to serve.

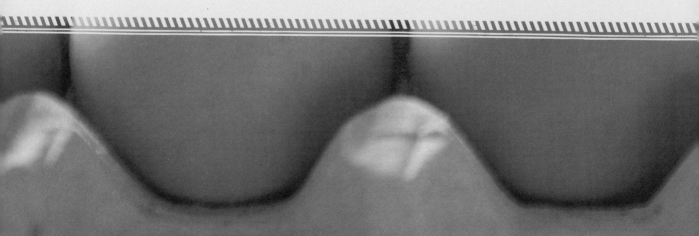

THAW

The sun rises a little earlier and burns just a little warmer every day as winter loosens its iron grip on our lives. Through crusts of snow, we peek at the promise of grass as we look for watercress along the icy beds of rushing creeks. We're weary of storage crops and ready for lighter fare. Patience eludes us: we're grateful for frozen vegetables, for fruit flown in from far-off shores. This is the cook's most challenging season, one that sparks creativity born of necessity. Happily, the first real crop of spring appears during Thaw—maple syrup. How fitting that it is our favorite sweet! Just a drizzle lifts pork roasts and squash mash and gives flavor and body to sauces and desserts. Once maple sap begins to flow, we know all the bright and lively things of spring are on their way.

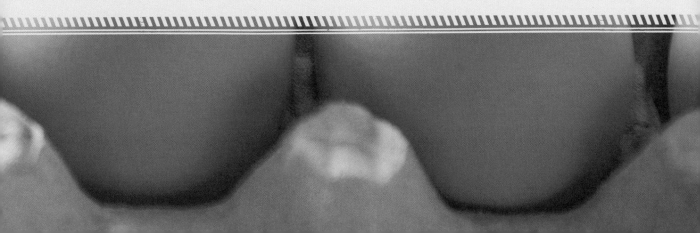

Surly Maple Braised
Pork Belly Benedict Serves 2 to 4

Let's get real: pork belly is simply uncured, unsmoked bacon, and it's
as lush and delicious as any cut of pork. It requires a long cooking time
to render the fat and turn the meat silky, unctuous, and tender. You can
cook the pork belly ahead of time and assemble the eggs Benedict the
next day. Braising the pork belly takes a good three to four hours. If you
have leftovers, save them for sandwiches and salads.

Pork Belly

1 pound pork belly

¼ cup packed dark brown sugar

Salt and freshly ground black pepper

4 cups Surly Furious, or your favorite
full-bodied brew

½ cup maple syrup

Marinated Kale

1 small bunch kale, tough ribs
removed and leaves sliced
(2 cups)

¼ cup Orange Honey Vinaigrette
(page 234)

Chipotle Hollandaise

¼ pound (1 stick) unsalted butter

3 egg yolks

2 tablespoons hot water

1 tablespoon fresh lemon juice

⅛ teaspoon salt

½ teaspoon ground chipotle,
or to taste

Poached Eggs

2 tablespoons white wine vinegar

Salt

4 large eggs

2 English muffins, split and toasted

Salt and freshly ground black pepper

Chopped parsley

continued on page 192

Wood's Maple Orchard
Elmwood, Wisconsin

The Wood family has been making award-winning syrup in its hauntingly beautiful forest for five generations. The family business, now run by **Steven and Dawn Wood**, and their son Jason, was founded in the 1840s when the family moved to the Midwest from northwestern New York. The Woods' sugar shack is on the premises, so the sap goes straight to processing: it's about as light and fresh as good syrup can ever get. Wood's Maple Syrup is one of the largest maple syrup producers in the region and continues to rely on time-tested methods to make syrup. It's a quick one-hour drive to the Woods' woods, and we're grateful that such sweet beauty exists nearby.

continued from page 188

Set the pork belly on a baking sheet. Rub the brown sugar and salt and pepper into the meat side of the belly. Heat a Dutch oven or a large heavy pot over medium-high heat and set the belly skin-side down in the Dutch oven. Sear until the fat is crispy and slightly rendered, about 5 to 7 minutes. Flip the pork belly, and sear the other side. Stir in the beer and the maple syrup. Bring the liquid to a boil, partially cover, and turn the heat to low, so the liquid is gently simmering. Continue simmering, turning the meat every hour or so and adding water if necessary. Continue cooking until the meat is very tender, about 4 hours. Allow the meat to rest before slicing it. (You may have leftovers; save them for sandwiches and salads.)

Cut 8 slices of the pork belly. Heat a skillet set over medium heat, and brown the meat on both sides, about 3 minutes per side.

Marinate the kale. Put the kale in a small bowl, and toss it with the Orange Honey Vinaigrette. Set the kale aside.

To make the chipotle hollandaise, melt the butter in a small saucepan over medium-low heat until it's foamy, about 5 minutes. In a small bowl, whisk together the egg yolks, hot water, lemon juice, and salt. Transfer the egg mixture to a food processor fitted with a metal blade. With the food processor running on high, slowly add the melted butter. Add the ground chipotle, and adjust the seasoning. Use immediately.

To poach the eggs, put 1 ½ inches of water in a skillet. Add the vinegar, and bring the water to a gentle simmer over medium-high heat. Reduce the heat. One by one, crack the eggs into a ramekin or a small bowl and gently slide each one into the simmering water. Poach the eggs until the whites are set and the yolks are runny, about 2 to 3 minutes. Use a slotted spoon to remove the eggs from the water, and place them on a towel-lined plate to drain. Lightly sprinkle the eggs with salt.

To assemble the eggs Benedict, place some kale on each English muffin half. Place two slices of seared pork belly on top of the kale. Place the poached egg on top of the pork. Top with a hefty drizzle of the chipotle hollandaise, sprinkle on some parsley, and season with salt and pepper.

Sweet Potato, Brown Rice, and Kale Savory Waffle Serves 6 to 8

We served these hearty savory waffles at our pop-up breakfast at Verdant Tea, Birchwood's Seward neighbor, while the cafe was being remodeled. Satisfying and super easy, they make a great dinner entrée too. Feel free to substitute squash for the sweet potatoes. Serve garnished with Cilantro Butter and Kumquat Honey Preserves.

4 medium sweet potatoes
¼ cup brown rice
2 cups unbleached all-purpose flour
1 tablespoon baking powder
½ teaspoon salt
1 cup milk

6 large eggs
3 leaves kale, tough stems removed
  and leaves shredded (½ cup)
Rice bran oil
Cilantro Butter (page 88)

Preheat the oven to 375 degrees. Prick the sweet potatoes all over with a fork and put them in the oven. Roast the sweet potatoes until they are very tender, about 45 minutes, or longer, depending on their size. Allow the sweet potatoes to cool. Peel the sweet potatoes, put them into a medium bowl, and mash until smooth.

Put the rice and a pinch of salt in a small pot with ¾ cup of water. Bring the water to a boil over high heat; then reduce it to a simmer, cover the pot, and cook for about 40 minutes. Remove from the heat, and set the covered pot aside for 10 minutes. Uncover the rice and fluff it with a fork.

In a large bowl, whisk together the flour, baking powder, and salt.

In a medium bowl, whisk together the milk and the eggs. Stir the egg mixture into the sweet potatoes. Gradually stir the sweet potato mixture into the flour. Stir in the brown rice and kale.

Reduce the oven temperature to 200 degrees. Heat up the waffle iron and lightly brush the cooking surfaces with oil. When the waffle iron is ready, pour in 1 cup of batter. Cook until the waffle is lightly browned, about 5 to 6 minutes. Transfer the waffle to a baking sheet and keep it warm, un-covered, in the oven until ready to serve. Repeat with the remaining batter.

Serve the waffles with a dollop of Cilantro Butter.

Poached Garlic and Cauliflower Soup (V) GF Serves 4 to 6

This recipe was developed for a chef demo we did at the Minnesota Garlic Festival, an annual county-fair fundraiser for the Sustainable Farming Association. Lush and light, this is a soup with plenty of flavor from the poached garlic. It's creamy, but contains no cream. Garnish the soup with Basil Oil and toasted chopped pistachios, and serve it with a hunk of hearty bread. Poach the garlic ahead of time, and be sure to reserve the oil.

4 heads garlic, separated into cloves and peeled

2 cups plus 1 tablespoon rice bran oil

1 head cauliflower, florets sliced into ½-inch pieces (3 cups)

8 cups vegetable stock

½ cup white wine

2 tablespoons lemon juice

1 tablespoon Dijon mustard

1 teaspoon cumin

1 teaspoon coriander

1 teaspoon sambal, or more to taste

Salt and freshly ground black pepper

Basil Oil (page 227)

Toasted pistachios

To make the poached garlic, put the garlic into a small saucepan, and cover it with 2 cups of the oil. Set the pan over low heat, and bring the oil to a gentle simmer. Simmer until the cloves are golden and very soft when pressed with a fork, about 50 minutes to 1 hour. Allow the garlic to cool in the oil.

Strain the garlic, and reserve the oil for future use. Be sure to store the oil in the refrigerator.

Preheat the oven to 375 degrees. Put the cauliflower into a large bowl, and toss it with 1 tablespoon of oil. Spread out the cauliflower on a baking sheet and roast it, shaking the pan occasionally, until it's nicely browned, about 25 to 25 minutes.

Turn the cauliflower and the garlic into a large soup pot, and add the stock, white wine, lemon juice, mustard, cumin, coriander, and sambal. Set the pot over medium-high heat, and bring the soup to a simmer. Reduce the heat, and cook until all the ingredients are very soft, about 20 minutes. Puree the soup with an immersion blender or, working in batches, in a blender. Season to taste with salt and pepper. Serve the soup garnished with Basil Oil and toasted pistachios.

Sausage Pizza Serves 6 to 8

This simple and humble pizza is a favorite among high school students who come in starving after school. At the Birchwood, we make our own sausage patties. Look for excellent sausages at co-ops and local meat markets, such as Clancey's Meats and Fish in Linden Hills.

1 pound sausage

Cornmeal for the peel

Birchwood Pizza and Flatbread
  Dough (page 147)

½ cup Tomato Fennel Ragout
  (page 198)

½ cup shredded mozzarella cheese

¼ cup shredded Parmesan cheese

1 to 2 tablespoons Basil Oil
  (page 227)

Crumble the sausage into a large skillet. Set the skillet over high heat, and cook, stirring, until the sausage is no longer pink, about 5 to 10 minutes. Remove the pan from the heat, and set it aside.

Preheat the oven to 425 degrees. Dust a pizza peel or a rimless baking sheet with cornmeal. On a lightly floured surface, roll out the dough into a 9- to 10-inch circle and place it on the pizza peel. Spread the Tomato Fennel Ragout over the dough.

Arrange the cooked sausage over the ragout. Sprinkle the mozzarella and Parmesan cheeses over the sausage. Gently shake the peel back and forth to make sure the crust is not sticking; then transfer the crust to the oven rack. Bake until the crust is nicely browned and the cheeses are bubbly, about 15 to 20 minutes. Drizzle Basil Oil over the pizza before serving it.

Tomato Fennel Ragout (V) GF Makes 4 cups

This is our house pizza sauce, and it's also great tossed with pasta or spooned over sausages on a crusty bun. Spiked with plenty of fennel seed and lots of rosemary, the sauce tastes even better a day or two after it's made. This recipe is easily doubled and freezes nicely.

2 tablespoons extra-virgin olive oil

1 large red onion, thinly sliced

1 large fennel bulb, thinly sliced

1 teaspoon fennel seeds, crushed

½ cup red wine

2 cups canned tomatoes, with their juices

½ teaspoon crushed red pepper, or more to taste

1 tablespoon thyme leaves

1 tablespoon chopped rosemary

Salt and freshly ground black pepper

Heat the oil in a large heavy pot, and sauté the onion and the fennel until they are soft, about 5 minutes. Stir in the fennel seeds and the red wine. Add the tomatoes, red pepper, thyme, and rosemary. Bring the sauce to a simmer, and cook, partially covered, until the flavors meld, about 30 minutes. Transfer the sauce to a blender and pulse it. Don't puree the sauce—it's meant to be chunky, not smooth.

Birchwood Turkey Burger with Rosemary-Lemon Mascarpone

Serves 4

In this recipe, the burger gets a nice lift from the tangy mascarpone. Try this spread on sandwiches and wraps too.

Rosemary-Lemon Mascarpone

1 cup mascarpone cheese

1 tablespoon chopped rosemary

1 tablespoon lemon juice, or more to taste

Turkey Burgers

1 tablespoon extra-virgin olive oil

2 cloves garlic, chopped

1 large shallot, chopped

1 stalk celery, leaves included, chopped

1 ⅓ pounds ground turkey

1 teaspoon ground pepper

1 teaspoon salt

Rice bran oil for frying the burgers

¼ pound shaved ham

¼ cup Pickled Red Onions (page 226)

1 cup microgreens

4 of your favorite buns

For the Rosemary-Lemon Mascarpone, beat the mascarpone with the rosemary and the lemon juice until smooth. Set aside.

Heat the olive oil in a small skillet set over medium heat. Add the garlic, shallot, and celery, and sauté until soft, about 2 minutes.

Put the ground turkey in a medium bowl, and work in the sautéed vegetables and the salt and pepper. Portion out 4 burgers and form them into patties. With your thumb, press a dimple into the middle of each patty.

continued on page 200

continued from page 199

To cook the burgers, heat a large skillet or griddle and brush it with oil. Fry the burgers until they are cooked through, about 5 minutes per side. The meat should register 165 degrees on a meat thermometer.

Spread a thick layer of the Rosemary-Lemon Mascarpone on the bottom halves of the buns. Set the turkey burgers on top, arrange the shaved ham on top of the burgers, and then add the pickled onions, the microgreens, and a dollop of Blue Cheese Ranch Mayo (page 241) before putting on the top halves of the buns.

Honey Almond Bars Makes about 24 bars

We buy local honey from Garden Farme and Ames. They help protect our pollinators, and we need healthy bees for healthy food and healthy lives.

Shortbread Base

1 ¼ cups unbleached all-purpose flour

2 tablespoons sugar

½ teaspoon baking powder

¼ teaspoon salt

8 tablespoons (1 stick) cold unsalted butter, cut into pieces

1 large egg

Topping

⅓ cup honey

¼ cup packed brown sugar

Pinch of salt

4 tablespoons (½ stick) cold unsalted butter, cut into pieces

1 ½ cups slivered almonds

Preheat the oven to 350 degrees. Butter a 9- or 10-inch-square baking pan, and line it with parchment paper, letting the paper rise above the sides. Butter the parchment paper.

Stir together the flour, sugar, baking powder, and salt. Cut in the butter with your fingertips or a pastry blender until the mixture resembles a coarse meal with small pea-sized butter lumps. Add the egg, and stir with a fork until the dough is crumbly.

Press the dough evenly into the bottom of the baking pan. Bake until the edges are golden and begin to pull away from the sides of the pan, about 15 to 20 minutes. Set the pan on a wire rack while you prepare the topping.

To make the topping, put the honey, brown sugar, and salt in a heavy saucepan and set it over medium heat. Bring the mixture to a boil, and stir until the sugar is dissolved, about 2 minutes. Stir in the butter, and return the mixture to a boil. Boil, stirring, for 1 minute. Remove the pan from the heat, and stir in the almonds. Pour the mixture over the warm pastry crust, spreading it evenly, and bake in the middle of the oven until the topping is caramelized and bubbling, 12 to 15 minutes. Place the pan on a rack, and let the bars cool completely. Use the parchment paper to lift the dessert out of the pan, and cut it into bars.

Heartbeet Farm
Zumbro Falls, Minnesota

Standing in the lush, bucolic fields of Heartbeet Farm, you'd never guess that you are only sixty miles south of Birchwood and the hustle and bustle of the city. Heartbeet is owned and operated by **Joe and Rebecca Schwen**, who grow the most beautiful hakurei turnips, chioggia beets, and shisho we have ever seen. They say the beauty of their produce is a "reflection of their desire to live a handmade life." Hosts of our monthly employee crop mobs, the Schwens love giving our staff a true hands-on connection to the land where our food comes from.

Heartbeet belongs to Full Circle Organic Growers Co-operative, which was founded by Joe's father, Stephen Schwen. Begun in 1985, this farmer co-op hosted organic farming conferences that eventually evolved into the annual MOSES (Midwest Organic and Sustainable Education Service) Organic Farming Conference. Today, Full Circle works with six organic farms to deliver produce throughout eastern Minnesota.

The Schwens work hard to keep Heartbeet's farming practices as sustainable as possible. They use a team of Percheron horses for much of the fieldwork; practice soil balancing to curb erosion; and farm at a "human scale." Farming is their life passion and also a family affair— if Joe and Rebecca are in the fields, you know their two children, Silas and Hazel, can't be far behind!

Sunny Day Sandwich (V) Serves 4

Especially at this time of year, a Sunny Day Sandwich just sounds promising. Our Sunflower Seed Spread makes a great dip and a nice alternative to cheese on a pizza. It will keep up to a week in the refrigerator. This combo sandwiches our Sunflower Seed Spread and roasted golden beets with roasted pears and microgreens.

Sunflower Seed Spread

1 cup roasted sunflower seeds

2 tablespoons coarsely chopped red onion

1 clove garlic, coarsely chopped

¼ cup coarsely chopped parsley

2 tablespoons lemon juice

2 teaspoons soy sauce, or more to taste

1 tablespoon maple syrup

2 tablespoons water, or more as needed

Salt and freshly ground black pepper

2 large pears, halved and cored

1 teaspoon sugar

1 teaspoon salt

One large golden beet, roasted and peeled

1 cup microgreens

8 slices of your favorite sandwich bread

To make the Sunflower Seed Spread, put the sunflower seeds, onion, garlic, parsley, lemon juice, soy sauce, and maple syrup into a food processor fitted with a steel blade. Process, adding water as needed to make a chunky puree. Season to taste with salt and pepper.

To roast the pears, preheat the oven to 350 degrees. Place some parchment paper on a baking sheet. Sprinkle the pears with a little sugar and salt. Place the pears cut-side down on the parchment paper, and roast until they are tender and slightly browned, about 25 to 30 minutes. When they are cool enough to handle, thinly slice the pears.

To assemble the sandwich, spread four slices of bread with the sunflower spread. Layer on a pear slice, a slice of golden beet, and microgreens. Top the sandwiches with the remaining slices of bread.

Green Curry with Tofu (V) GF
or Fish GF Serves 4 to 6

This vibrant green curry works beautifully with chunks of a mild fish—
tilapia, perch, or whitefish—or with tofu. Traditionally, green curry
tends to be more pungent than the milder red curries. It freezes nicely
and is good to have on hand. At the Birchwood, we serve this curry over
brown rice with grilled tangerine or lemon slices and nuts, and garnish
it with frizzled beets.

2 teaspoons coriander seeds

2 teaspoons green peppercorns

2 teaspoons cumin seeds

½ cinnamon stick, broken

1 star anise, broken

1 small shallot, coarsely chopped

2 to 3 Thai peppers or 4 to 6
jalapeños, seeded, veined, and
coarsely chopped

3 inches ginger, peeled and coarsely
chopped

3 garlic cloves, coarsely chopped

1 cup coarsely chopped cilantro
leaves and stems

2 teaspoons lime zest

2 tablespoons fresh lime juice

2 tablespoons coconut oil

1 onion, thinly sliced

1 parsnip or 1 carrot, thinly sliced

1 stalk celery, thinly sliced

2 cups coconut milk

1 tablespoon tamari

1 tablespoon maple syrup

1 tablespoon miso

1 (14-ounce) block tofu, drained
and cut into 1-inch or larger
pieces, or 1 pound mild white fish
filleted and cut into chunks

Put the coriander, peppercorns, cumin, cinnamon, and anise in a small,
dry skillet, and toast the spices over medium heat until they're fragrant,
about 30 seconds. Use a grinder to grind the spices into a fine powder.
Sift the ground spices to ensure there are no chunks.

Put the shallot, peppers, ginger, garlic, cilantro, lime zest, and lime juice
into a food processor fitted with a steel blade. Process into a paste. Stir
in the spices to make a curry paste.

Heat the coconut oil in a large, heavy skillet. Sauté the onions, parsnips,
and celery until softened, about 5 minutes. Stir in the curry paste, and
cook for another 30 seconds. Stir in the coconut milk, tamari, maple
syrup, and miso, and bring the curry to a simmer. Add the tofu or fish,
and cook until thoroughly heated through, about 5 to 8 minutes.

Glazed Grapefruit Bread Makes 1 loaf

Great with coffee, even better with tea, this bread stays moist and toasts nicely.

1 ½ cups unbleached all-purpose flour

2 teaspoons baking powder

½ teaspoon salt

1 cup plain yogurt

1 cup sugar

3 large eggs

Grated zest of 1 small grapefruit

½ teaspoon vanilla extract

½ cup rice bran oil

1 cup powdered sugar

3 tablespoons freshly squeezed grapefruit juice

Preheat the oven to 325 degrees. Lightly grease an 8 ½ × 4 ½-inch loaf pan.

In a medium bowl, whisk together the flour, baking powder, and salt. In a separate bowl, beat together the yogurt, sugar, eggs, grapefruit zest, and vanilla. Whisk in the oil. Add the dry ingredients to the wet ingredients, and stir until just combined. Pour the batter into the prepared pan, and bake until a toothpick inserted in the center comes out clean, about 55 to 65 minutes.

To make the glaze, whisk together the powdered sugar and the grapefruit juice. Pour the glaze over the top of the loaf while it is still warm. Use a spatula to evenly distribute the glaze.

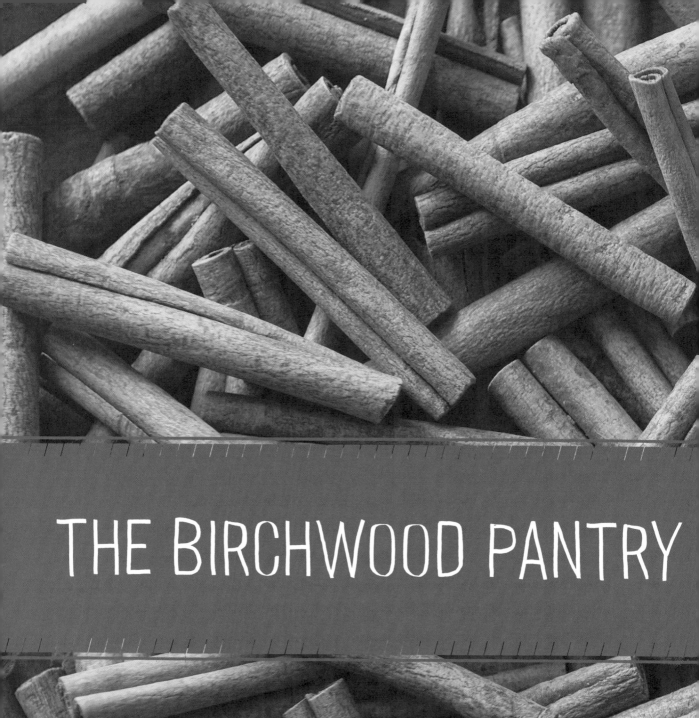

THE BIRCHWOOD PANTRY

Here's where we store Birchwood's magic. Just a dollop of this or a drizzle of that can perk up the simplest plate. Most of these condiments can be made ahead and kept on hand. Stock up!

PRESERVES

Jam, jelly, marmalade, chutney, sweet, savory, or spicy—preserves work wonders in a range of dishes. These recipes are for small batches that are quick and easy to make and best enjoyed right away. Store them in the refrigerator; there's no need to process or can them if covered in the refrigerator and served within a few months.

Rhubarb Strawberry Jam Makes 5 pints

1 ½ pounds rhubarb, cut into
½-inch pieces (5 cups)
6 cups sugar

¼ cup lemon juice
1 ½ pounds strawberries, hulled, big
berries halved (5 cups)

In a large, heavy pot, mix the rhubarb with the sugar and let it stand for two hours, or overnight. Stir in the lemon juice and the strawberries. Set the pot over high heat and bring the jam to a boil, stirring to dissolve the sugar. Reduce the heat and simmer, stirring occasionally, until the jam thickens enough to coat the back of a spoon, about 15 to 25 minutes. A candy thermometer inserted into the middle of the jam should read 220 degrees.

Remove the pan from the heat, skim off any foam, and ladle the jam into sterilized jars. Cover and cool the jars before storing them in the refrigerator.

Cranberry Tangelo Jam

Makes about 4 to 6 half-pints

Spoon this soft jam over waffles, or swirl it into mayonnaise for a sandwich spread or a dressing.

5 to 6 tangelos, scrubbed

2 cups cranberries

1 cup honey

Bring a large pot of water to a boil over high heat. Pierce the tangelos with the tines of a fork. Place the tangelos in the boiling water for 10 seconds. Remove, and allow to cool.

Put the tangelos in the freezer for about 15 minutes. Using a mandolin or a very sharp knife, cut the chilled tangelos into ⅛-inch slices. Transfer the slices to a wide, shallow saucepan. Add the cranberries and the honey, stir, and set the pan over medium-low heat. Bring the mixture to a simmer, and cook until the tangelo slices become glossy and the liquid has reduced to a jam-like consistency, about 15 to 20 minutes. A candy thermometer inserted into the center of the pan should read 220 degrees.

Remove the pan from the heat, skim off any foam, and ladle the jam into sterilized jars. Cover and cool the jars before storing them in the refrigerator.

Blueberry Black Currant Jam

Makes about 5 to 6 half-pints

Blue Fruit Farm, near Winona, Minnesota, provides us with the most beautiful blue fruit. In this simple combination, the true rich flavor of the fruit shines through. Serve it on the Bacon Blueberry Black Currant Oatmeal (page 110) or slather it on toast. It's terrific spooned over pound cake and vanilla ice cream too.

4 pounds blueberries

1 cup black currants

2 tablespoons lemon juice

5 cups sugar

Stir together the fruit, lemon juice, and sugar in a mixing bowl. Let the fruit stand for about 1 hour at room temperature, or overnight.

Turn the fruit into a wide saucepan, set it over medium heat, and bring the jam to a simmer. For a smooth jam, puree the mixture with an immersion blender, or puree it in a blender and return it to the pan. Cook, stirring, over low heat until the mixture thickens, about 15 to 20 minutes. A candy thermometer inserted into the center of the pot should read 220 degrees.

Remove the pan from the heat, skim off any foam, and ladle the jam into sterilized jars. Cover and cool the jars before storing them in the refrigerator.

Rhubarb Jalapeño Marmalade

Makes 5 half-pints

Tart and spicy and sweet, this marmalade is great on our Asparagus, Cheddar, and Quinoa Savory Waffle (page 2), spread on sandwiches, and on a cheese plate.

1 ½ pounds rhubarb, cut into ½-inch pieces (5 cups)
6 ½ cups sugar
¼ cup fresh lime juice

4 jalapeños, seeded, veined, and chopped
Pinch of salt

In a large, heavy pot, mix the rhubarb with the sugar and let it stand for two hours, or overnight.

Stir in the lime juice and the jalapeños. Set the pot over high heat. Stir as the mixture comes to a boil. Reduce the heat, and stir in the salt. Simmer until the mixture thickens, about 15 to 20 minutes. A candy thermometer inserted into the center should read 220 degrees.

Remove the pan from the heat, and skim off any foam. Ladle the marmalade into sterilized jars. Cover and cool the jars before storing them in the refrigerator.

Pear Cranberry Chutney

Makes about 4 pints

We serve this alongside our Winter Vegetable Hand Pie (page 168) and as a condiment for our cheese plates, roast chicken, and curry. Make a big batch to have on hand and to share.

8 medium pears, peeled, cored, and diced

6 cups cranberries

1 cup red wine

Juice of 2 oranges, juiced orange halves reserved

1 cup apple cider

1 cup packed brown sugar

4 to 5 inches ginger, minced (¼ cup)

4 cloves garlic, minced

1 tablespoon cinnamon

1 teaspoon cloves

Salt and finely ground black pepper

Put the pears, cranberries, wine, orange juice, orange halves, apple cider, brown sugar, ginger, and garlic into a large pot. Add the cinnamon, cloves, and a little salt and pepper. Set the pot over low heat, and bring the contents to a simmer. Cook, stirring occasionally, until the mixture is very thick, about 20 to 30 minutes. Taste and adjust the seasoning. Remove the orange halves, and ladle the chutney into sterilized jars. Cover and cool the jars before storing them in the refrigerator.

Kumquat Honey Preserves

Makes about 1 pint

These preserves are wonderful as a sauce for chicken, pork, and duck.

2 pounds kumquats, washed,
halved, cut into thin strips, and
seeded

⅓ cup honey
⅓ cup water
Pinch of salt

Put the kumquats, honey, water, and a healthy pinch of salt into a large pot. Bring the preserves to a simmer over medium heat; then reduce the temperature to low. Simmer for 20 to 30 minutes, stirring often, until the kumquat skins have softened and the mixture thickens. A candy thermometer inserted into the center should read 220 degrees.

Remove the pan from the heat, and skim off any foam. Ladle the preserves into sterilized jars. Cover and cool the jars before storing them in the refrigerator.

Cranberry Quince Chutney

Makes about 6 half-pints

This chutney is brilliant over the holidays, tart and mellow and so pretty on the holiday table. It also makes a terrific gift.

3 quince, peeled and diced
3 cups cranberries
½ cup port
½ cup orange juice
½ cup packed brown sugar
4 to 5 inches ginger, minced
(¼ cup)

1 orange, chopped, including the
rind, and its juice
1 cinnamon stick
¼ cup apple cider
1 tablespoon minced garlic
1 teaspoon cloves
Salt and freshly ground black pepper

Put all of the ingredients into a large pot, and bring the mixture to a boil. Reduce the heat to very low, and simmer until the mixture is thick and jammy, about 45 to 60 minutes.

Ladle the chutney into sterilized jars. Cover and cool the jars before storing them in the refrigerator.

Vanilla Extract Makes 1 cup

Vanilla extract makes a terrific gift when presented in a pretty bottle. It's easy to make, and easy to double or triple the recipe. This is the vanilla we use at the Birchwood; it's far tastier and much less expensive than any commercial brand. In the cafe, we use organic Madagascar vanilla beans and Prairie organic vodka.

1 (8-ounce) glass bottle or jar
5 vanilla beans

1 cup Prairie or other 80 proof good-quality vodka

Sterilize the bottle. Slice each vanilla bean lengthwise, and place it in the bottle. Pour in the vodka, making sure it covers the beans. Shake the bottle once a day over the course of eight weeks. Store at room temperature out of direct sunlight.

Meyer Lemon Syrup Makes 4 half-pints

Here's a light, tangy syrup that is great on waffles and whisked into vinaigrettes.

2 ½ pounds Meyer lemons

2 cups sugar

Juice the lemons, and measure out 2 ½ cups of juice. Pour the juice into a saucepan, and add the sugar. Set the pan over medium heat, and bring the liquid to a boil. Reduce the heat, and simmer, stirring, until the sugar melts, about 2 minutes.

Pour the syrup into sterilized jars. Cover and cool the jars before storing them in the refrigerator.

PICKLES, CONDIMENTS, AND OILS

Refrigerator Dill Pickles

Makes about 2 pints

We use these pickles to garnish everything. During the height of cucumber season, we have a pickle party, dedicating eight-hour shifts to pickling cukes.

5 to 6 pickling cucumbers (about 1 pound), sliced thin

6 sprigs fresh dill

4 cloves garlic, crushed, or 4 garlic scapes

1 ½ cups rice wine vinegar

¼ cup sugar

1 tablespoon salt

8 black peppercorns, lightly crushed

1 tablespoon coriander seeds

1 tablespoon sambal

Pack the cucumbers, dill, and garlic into sterilized glass jars. Put the vinegar, sugar, salt, peppercorns, coriander, and sambal into a saucepan, and bring the liquid to a boil over medium-high heat. Reduce the heat, cover, and simmer for 1 minute.

Pour the liquid over the cucumbers, and let it cool to room temperature. Cover the jars, and refrigerate the pickles. Marinate the cucumbers in the refrigerator for at least 2 days, shaking the jars occasionally, before serving.

Pickled Radishes Makes about 1 pint

Pickle your favorite radish as a condiment for grilled meats and fish and scrambled eggs. The gorgeous Beauty Heart radish, which has a shocking pink heart within a pale green exterior, makes a very pretty condiment.

1 pound radishes, sliced or diced
8 cloves garlic, peeled
2 teaspoons peppercorns
½ cup water

1 cup white wine vinegar
2 teaspoons salt
1 tablespoon honey

Put the radishes, garlic, and peppercorns into a sterilized glass jar. Put the water, vinegar, salt, and honey into a small saucepan, and bring the liquid to a boil. Remove the pan from the heat, and stir until the salt and honey are dissolved.

Pour the liquid over the radishes. Cover and cool the jar before storing it in the refrigerator. To allow the spices to marry, shake the jar every day for 3 days before using the pickles.

Pickled Peppers Makes about 2 pints

Pickled peppers add snap to pizzas and are great with burgers. They are loaded with heat, so be careful when handling them!

1 ½ pounds mixed chili peppers (Anaheim, jalapeño, serrano, hot banana)

4 cloves garlic, peeled

3 cups white wine vinegar

1 cup water

2 tablespoons coarse salt

2 tablespoons sugar

Cut the peppers into ½-inch rings, discard the stems, and remove the seeds. Pack the peppers and the garlic into sterilized jars. Put the vinegar, water, salt, and sugar into a saucepan, and bring the liquid to a boil over medium-high heat. Reduce the heat, cover the pan, and simmer for 1 minute.

Pour the liquid over the peppers, and let it cool to room temperature. Cover the jars, and refrigerate the pickles. Marinate the peppers in the refrigerator for at least 2 weeks, shaking the jars occasionally, before using.

Pickled Red Onions Makes about 2 pints

Serve pickled red onions on sandwiches, burgers, or pizza—anything that needs a lift!

1 large red onion, cut into ¼-inch slices

2 cloves garlic, peeled

1 cup apple cider vinegar

1 cup water

2 tablespoons sugar

2 teaspoons coarse salt

Pack the onions and the garlic into sterilized jars. Put the vinegar, water, sugar, and salt into a saucepan, and bring the liquid to a boil over medium-high heat. Reduce the heat and simmer, covered, for 1 minute.

Pour the liquid over the onions, and let it cool to room temperature. Cover the jars, and store them in the refrigerator.

Basil Oil Makes about ¾ cup

1 ½ cups fresh, clean basil leaves   1 cup extra-virgin olive oil

Blanch the basil leaves very briefly in rapidly boiling water. Drain the basil, then put the leaves into some cheesecloth and squeeze out as much water as possible.

Put the oil in a blender, and add the basil in batches so it is thoroughly pureed. Strain the mixture through a medium sieve, and then strain it again through a fine mesh strainer. Line a clean coffee cone or a colander with a paper filter and set it over a small bowl. Pour the strained oil into the coffee filter, cover, and set the whole rig in the refrigerator to strain overnight. Transfer the oil into a sterilized jar, and store it in the refrigerator.

Chili Oil Makes 1 cup

This is our go-to oil to finish roasted corn and cream soups and to brighten black bean dishes. Keep it on hand.

1 cup crushed red pepper   2 teaspoons salt
1 teaspoon cayenne   1 cup rice bran oil
2 teaspoons hot paprika

Put all of the ingredients into a blender and puree. Strain the oil through a fine mesh strainer.

Line a clean coffee cone with a filter, and set the cone over a small bowl. Pour the strained oil into the coffee filter, and allow it to drip overnight. Pour the oil into a sterilized glass jar. Cover the jar, and store it at room temperature.

Preserved Lemons Makes 1 quart

Preserved lemons are mellow yet intensely lemony—not nearly as sour or nose-tingly as fresh lemon. Rinse off the salt, scrape out the pulp, and use the peel, which is satiny: they make everything a little sweeter. You can pair these lemons with olives, chop and toss them into risotto or couscous, and create a lovely balance to sweet dried apricots and honey with preserved lemons served over chèvre.

Preserved lemons are so easy they really don't require a recipe, just patience to wait the month or so until they are ready. Be sure to use organic lemons because, after all, you're eating the peel.

4 lemons (see note)

4 tablespoons coarse sea salt

4 cinnamon sticks

4 whole cloves

4 coriander seeds

4 black peppercorns

2 bay leaves

4 additional lemons, or more, to be juiced as needed

Wash and scrub the lemons. Cut each lemon in quarters but not all the way through; the pieces should remain attached at the stem end. Stuff each lemon with a tablespoon of the salt. Put the spices into a sterilized jar; then add the lemons, pressing them down so that they are squashed together. Close the jar.

Leave the jar at room temperature for three days so the lemons release some of their juices. Open the jar and press the lemons down as much as you can, and then add fresh lemon juice to cover them entirely.

Close the jar, and leave the lemons in a cool place for about a month. The longer they are left, the better their flavor will be. If part of a lemon is not covered with juice, it will develop a white mold. (The mold is harmless; just rinse it off.) After opening the jar, store the preserved lemons in the refrigerator.

To use the lemons, remove and discard the pulp and run the lemon peel under cold running water to rinse off the salt.

WE PREFER MEYER LEMONS in this recipe. They have very thin skins and are less assertive than other varieties.

Roasted Meyer Lemon Oil

Makes about 1 ½ cups

Keep this oil on hand to drizzle over fish or chicken, finish a salad, or whisk into a vinaigrette. Store the oil at room temperature.

3 Meyer lemons, quartered and seeded

3 cups rice bran oil

Preheat the oven to 350 degrees. Line a baking sheet with parchment paper.

Set the lemons on the baking sheet, and roast them until they begin to brown, about 15 to 20 minutes.

Put the lemons and the oil into a blender and puree into a fine paste. Strain the paste first through a medium sieve and then through a fine mesh sieve. Line a clean coffee cone with a filter, and set it over a small bowl. Pour the mixture into the coffee filter, and allow it to drip overnight.

Place the oil in the freezer for exactly 45 minutes (no longer than that). Skim the frozen water off the top of the separated mixture. Pour the oil into a sterilized glass jar. Cover the jar, and store it at room temperature.

Horseradish Mustard Oil

Makes about 1½ cups

This oil packs a wallop, so use it with a light touch on green beans, smoked salmon, and chicken confit.

½ cup preserved horseradish
1 tablespoon whole grain mustard
1 tablespoon Dijon Mustard

1 cup rice bran oil
Salt and freshly ground black pepper

Puree all of the ingredients in a blender. Strain the oil through a fine mesh strainer.

Line a clean coffee cone with a filter, and set the cone over a small bowl. Pour the strained oil into the coffee filter, and allow it to drip overnight. Pour the oil into a sterilized glass jar. Cover the jar, and store it at room temperature.

PRESERVING HORSERADISH IS NOT FOR THE FAINT OF HEART!
Chef Marshall preserves Birchwood's horseradish for his recipes and to sell in the cafe.

VINAIGRETTES, SALAD DRESSINGS, AND SAUCES

Roasted Pear Vinaigrette Makes 1 cup

We use this dressing on our grain salads, on roasted beets, and tossed with dark greens.

2 pears, peeled, cored, and quartered

⅓ cup cider vinegar

2 teaspoons whole grain mustard

1 small shallot, minced

1 tablespoon thyme leaves

2 tablespoons honey

⅔ cup rice bran oil

Salt and freshly ground black pepper

Preheat the oven to 350 degrees. Line a baking sheet with parchment paper and lay the pears on the parchment. Roast the pears for 30 minutes; then turn them to coat them in their juices. Continue roasting until they are caramelized, about 25 to 30 more minutes.

Put the pears, vinegar, mustard, shallot, thyme, and honey into a blender. Puree, adding the oil in a slow, steady stream. Season with salt and pepper to taste. Store the vinaigrette in a sterilized jar, covered, in the refrigerator.

Horseradish Vinaigrette Makes about 1 cup

Drizzle this vinaigrette over smoked fish or smoked turkey and roasted root vegetables. Whisk it into sour cream for a dipping sauce.

¼ cup preserved horseradish, or more to taste
2 tablespoons chopped fresh dill
¼ cup rice wine vinegar

¼ cup lime juice
½ cup rice bran oil
Salt and freshly ground black pepper

Put the horseradish, dill, vinegar, and lime juice into a blender and puree until smooth. Slowly add the oil in a steady stream. Store the vinaigrette in a sterilized jar, covered, in the refrigerator.

Cranberry Vinaigrette Makes about 1 ½ cups

This lively vinaigrette is just right for our Apple and Alemar Salad (page 94) and is wonderful tossed into turkey salad or wild rice salad.

½ cup cranberries
1 small shallot, minced
1 teaspoon minced rosemary
2 tablespoons chopped parsley
1 tablespoon honey

2 tablespoons preserved horseradish
⅓ cup raspberry or white wine vinegar
⅔ cup rice bran oil
Salt and freshly ground black pepper

Put the cranberries, shallot, rosemary, parsley, honey, horseradish, and vinegar into a blender. Puree, adding the oil in a slow, steady stream. Season to taste with salt and pepper. Store the vinaigrette in a sterilized jar, covered, in the refrigerator.

Orange Honey Vinaigrette

Makes about 1 ½ cups

Sweet and tart, this vinaigrette is especially good in turkey salad or drizzled over roast pork with grilled vegetables. It will keep several days in the refrigerator.

¼ cup orange juice
¼ cup white wine vinegar
2 tablespoons honey
1 tablespoon chopped shallot

1 clove garlic, minced
1 teaspoon coriander
½ cup rice bran oil
Salt and freshly ground black pepper

Put the orange juice, vinegar, honey, shallot, garlic, coriander, and oil into a blender and process until smooth. Season to taste with salt and pepper. Store the vinaigrette in a sterilized jar, covered, in the refrigerator.

Green Tea Vinaigrette Makes 1 cup

When matcha was the surprise ingredient in a chef's challenge, Marshall was inspired to create this vinaigrette on the spot. We liked it so much that it's now a standard on our Spring menu. We use it liberally in the Spring Egg Scramble (page 3), Spring Vegetable Pizza (page 14), and many of our salads and vegetable stir-fries.

1 tablespoon matcha (green tea powder)
⅓ cup rice wine vinegar
½ cup mint leaves
2 teaspoons Dijon mustard

1 teaspoon lime juice
1 tablespoon maple syrup
1 clove garlic, smashed
1 tablespoon chopped shallot
⅓ cup rice bran oil

Heat the tea and the vinegar in a small saucepan, and allow it to steep for about 5 minutes. Let the mixture cool.

Put the steeped tea, mint, mustard, lime juice, maple syrup, garlic, and shallot into a blender. Puree, adding the oil in a slow, steady stream. Store the vinaigrette in a sterilized jar, covered, in the refrigerator. Use it within a week.

Strawberry White Balsamic Vinaigrette Makes about 1 cup

This vinaigrette is a must on our Strawberry Salad with Garlic Chèvre Mousse (page 34) and is delicious on grilled asparagus.

¼ cup white balsamic vinegar
1 small shallot, minced
2 teaspoons prepared mustard
½ teaspoon pink peppercorns

1 teaspoon sugar
¼ cup mashed strawberries
½ cup rice bran oil
Salt and freshly ground black pepper

Put the vinegar, shallot, mustard, peppercorns, sugar, and strawberries into a blender. Puree, adding the oil in a slow, steady stream. Season to taste with salt and pepper. Store the vinaigrette in a sterilized jar, covered, in the refrigerator. Use it within 3 days.

Sesame Tamari Vinaigrette

Makes 1 cup

This vinaigrette is great on the Sesame Green Bean and Quinoa Salad (page 39) and on rice noodle salads. It also makes a terrific dip for veggies.

1 jalapeño, seeded, veined, and minced

1 garlic clove, minced

2 tablespoons fish sauce

2 teaspoons honey

¼ cup lime juice

2 tablespoons dark sesame oil

2 tablespoons tamari

½ cup rice bran oil

Put the jalapeño, garlic, fish sauce, honey, lime juice, sesame oil, and tamari into a blender. Puree, adding the oil in a slow, steady stream. Store the vinaigrette in a sterilized jar, covered, in the refrigerator.

Poached Garlic and Honey Vinaigrette Makes about 1 ½ cups

This is a must on the Heirloom Tomato Plate (page 64) and is delicious drizzled over roasted corn. Poaching the garlic in olive oil mellows the cloves and yields a lovely flavored oil to use in dressings and sauces.

¼ cup garlic cloves
1 cup extra-virgin olive oil
Pinch of turmeric

¼ cup honey
½ cup cider vinegar
Salt and freshly ground pepper

Put the garlic cloves and the olive oil in a small saucepan set over low heat, and simmer for 20 minutes. Allow the oil to cool to room temperature. Remove the garlic cloves, and transfer the garlic oil to a sterilized glass jar.

Put the poached garlic cloves, turmeric, honey, and vinegar in a blender. Process, adding ½ cup of the reserved garlic oil in a slow, steady stream. Store the vinaigrette in a sterilized jar in the refrigerator. Also refrigerate the remaining garlic oil (see note).

USE THE REMAINING GARLIC-INFUSED OLIVE OIL for drizzling over grilled steak, seasoning cold soups, and on grilled vegetables.

Birchwood Aioli (with variations)

Makes 1 cup

THERE ARE LEGITIMATE CONCERNS ABOUT USING RAW EGGS that we do not take lightly. We are careful to use only organic, free-range eggs from our friends on local farms who employ best practices to ensure that the chickens are well cared for and the eggs are handled properly. You may substitute a good-quality mayonnaise for Birchwood Aioli in any of our recipes.

We use aioli as a base for sandwich spreads and dips.

4 cloves garlic, peeled
2 egg yolks (see note)
1 tablespoon lemon juice

1 teaspoon Dijon mustard
½ cup rice bran oil
Salt and freshly ground white pepper

In a food processor fitted with a metal blade, puree the garlic, egg yolks, lemon juice, and mustard. With the processor running on high, add the oil slowly, drop by drop, until you have a mayo. Season with salt and white pepper to taste. Store the aioli, covered, in the refrigerator for up to a week.

Aioli Variations

We serve Roasted Jalapeño Aioli on our Black Bean Quinoa Burger (page 77). Basil Pesto Aioli is a must-have on the Heirloom Tomato Sweet Corn BLT (page 69) and on any sandwich with tomatoes for that matter. Toss it with cold pasta for a pasta salad.

To make these variations, whisk the listed ingredients into a half-cup of aioli.

Roasted Jalapeño Aioli

2 tablespoon lime juice plus 1 jalapeño, roasted, seeded, and chopped

Basil Pesto Aioli

2 tablespoons Arugula Basil Pesto (page 12)

Anaheim Chili Sauce Makes 2 ½ cups

This is hot stuff, so be super careful handling the peppers. When working with peppers, we wear gloves and do not touch our eyes. Drizzle the sauce over burgers, tacos, and pizzas.

1 tablespoon extra-virgin olive oil

1 jalapeño, stemmed, seeded, and chopped

2 Anaheim or Santa Fe peppers, stemmed, seeded, and chopped

2 cloves garlic, minced

2 stalks celery, diced

¼ cup diced onion

2 cups canned tomatoes, with their juice

2 teaspoons cider vinegar

2 teaspoons sambal, or more to taste

Salt and freshly ground black pepper

Heat the oil in a heavy saucepan set over medium heat, and sauté the peppers, garlic, celery, and onion until soft, about 3 to 5 minutes. Stir in the tomatoes, vinegar, and sambal. Reduce the heat, and simmer until the sauce is thick, about 20 to 30 minutes. Season to taste with salt and pepper. Store the sauce in a sterilized jar, covered, in the refrigerator. Use it within 3 weeks.

Blue Cheese Ranch Mayo Makes 1 ½ cups

Try this on grilled steak and spread on roast beef sandwiches. It also makes a great dip.

½ cup buttermilk
¾ cup blue cheese
¾ cup mayonnaise
1 tablespoon cider vinegar
1 teaspoon prepared mustard

¼ cup chopped fresh dill
½ cup chopped parsley
1 teaspoon sugar, or to taste
Salt and freshly ground black pepper

In a medium bowl, whisk together the buttermilk, blue cheese, mayonnaise, vinegar, mustard, dill, and parsley. Add sugar to taste, and season with salt and pepper. Store the mayo, covered, in the refrigerator for up to five days.

Birchwood Ketchup Makes 1 ½ cups

This is essential with French Fries! In creating this recipe, Marshall wanted to replicate the flavor of his favorite brand of ketchup from childhood but with better, cleaner organic ingredients and no artificial colors or preservatives.

1 (6-ounce) can tomato paste
½ cup organic light corn syrup
½ cup white vinegar
¼ cup water

1 tablespoon sugar
1 teaspoon salt
¼ teaspoon onion powder
⅛ teaspoon garlic powder

Place all ingredients into a blender. Puree on high until a vortex forms and the ketchup is ultra-smooth and glossy.

Acknowledgments

"Innumerable measures bring us this food, we should know how it comes to us"
—ZEN MEAL PRAYER

Just as innumerable measures bring us our food, innumerable people have graced my path at just the right moment so that I could share the Birchwood Cafe, and now this book, with you. My list is long, but here is a start: thanks to Susan Muskat, Bill Dickinson, Bridget Ferguson, Jean Garbarini, Pat Pratt, Karen Peterson, Joy Teiken, Bob Fuchs, Kristen Arden, Kim Knutson, Jennifer Blair, William Prottengeier, Patti Lombardo, Karl Benson, Patrick O'Brien, Beth Parkhill, Helene Murray, Wynne Yelland, Ali Selim, Mary Mccallum, Christine Weeks, Diane Nunberg, Peggy Rasmussen, and Nichole Goodwell. Each in your own way, you inspired me to take that next step even when I couldn't see the road ahead.

Connecting to our food connects us to our own source, and food and hospitality are in my DNA. I thank my Mom and Dad for my innate urge to care for others with food. To my great-grandma "Nanny" I give thanks for my earliest memories of love, comfort, and good, real food. To grandma "Mema": I now appreciate your zero tolerance of my childhood complaints; your words, "If you don't like something, do something about it," became my mantra when I realized just how broken the prevailing food system really is.

Every day I thank my lucky stars for Lucia Watson. I thank her for hiring me, for reintroducing me to good, real food, and for creating a new paradigm for how restaurants can and should work. I've done my best to follow in her food steps: sourcing from people and places we know and trust, and creating and serving food with love and care in a manner that fosters respect for each other and nourishes both staff and community.

Thank you to Cy and Del Bursch for taking your time to decide and trusting us to carry on the Birchwood legacy.

I'm grateful to Will Allen for insisting I bring the movie *Fresh* to the Twin Cities. This hopeful and inspiring film by Ana Joanes ignited our local food movement as well as my own advocacy. We promise a lifetime of Chocolate Crinkle Cookies!

Our farmers and producers are the true unsung heroes who toil tirelessly to bring us our food, all the while caring for the people, the animals, and the planet. The fruits of your labor are the inspiration for Good Real Food, and our relationships with you are what make all the hard work worthwhile.

Speaking of heroes, a huge hug of thanks to Greg Reynolds (MOSES 2015 Organic Farmer of the Year)—whom I adore teasing at every opportunity—for these many years of friendship and collaboration. You've done so much to connect our community to where their food comes from. If only all kids could grow up like Lily, with their very own farmer. Let's make it so!

Words cannot express my gratitude and appreciation for our amazing, hardworking team of talented chefs, bakers, dishwashers, admin support, and front-of-house servers, past and present. I feel so fortunate I get to work alongside you all. The pride and dedication each and every one of you brings to the creation and service of Good Real Food is at the

heart of what the Birchwood is really all about.

And Chef! A very special thank you to Marshall Paulsen, a man I'm honored to call my friend. There have been many days when the door and other opportunities beckoned, and yet he stayed. It tickles me to no end that Amanda calls me the best "work wife" a chef's wife could ask for. And why do I love Marshall's mom? Because savory waffle!

To my business partner, Steve Davidson, I bow in namaste.

To my dear friend Mette Nielsen, our talented photographer, for crafting the idea and holding the vision for this book over these many years, and to her partner in culinary creativity, the accomplished author and local food guru Beth Dooley. I love you both! Your guidance, patience, and perseverance have conspired to bring this book to life.

A special thank you to our copy editor, Pam Price, for her inspired suggestions, eagle eye, and careful attention to every detail in this book, and our deepest thanks to Abigail Wyckoff for her artistry and imagination in styling the food for photography. We are also grateful for the expertise of Daniel Ochsner, who managed the design and production of the cookbook at the University of Minnesota Press; the editorial advice and direction of Erik Anderson; and the engagement and artistic talents of designer Brian Donahue.

A very loud shout-out to our 980 Kickstarter backers, especially Hungry Turtle Farmers Coop, Bill Davnie, John Levy, Geoffroy Noonan and Kendra Cornwall, Marian Rubenfeld, Wendy Hurd, and John and Michele Stangl. Your support allowed us to #growbirchwoodgrow.

And finally, I thank our customers, the key ingredient of this vast, deep, and delicious community we've all created together. Thank you for joining me on the path to Good Real Food. Your loyal patronage and unwavering support these past twenty years fuels our quest to create a better food system and powers my purpose to connect people to their food. May the journey continue!

—*Tracy Singleton*

• • •

Thank you to Tracy for providing all of us with a home in which to put our creativity and passion to good use these past twenty years.

Thank you to Blanca, Bridget, Dan, Hudson, Kristi, Lourdes, Matt, Nancy, Peter, Sandra, Thaddeus, Trevor, Zach, and every other cook with whom I have had and continue to have the honor of creating Good Real Food at Birchwood. These recipes are all of ours.

And to Richard, Jane, Mark, Colin, and Wes for igniting my interest in good, real food.

And to my mom for feeding me waffles with bacon and eggs.

And, of course, to my secret sous chef: you know who you are.

—*Marshall Paulsen*

Index

Tracy Singleton has been at the forefront of local food in the Twin Cities for almost two decades. She launched the Birchwood Cafe in 1995 with a vision of serving locally sourced, fresh, flavorful food and encouraging engaged community involvement. Over the past twenty years, the restaurant has been a culinary favorite in the Seward neighborhood of Minneapolis.

Marshall Paulsen has been the executive chef at Birchwood Cafe since 2006. He lives in St. Paul with his wife and daughter.

Beth Dooley has been writing about local food for the past twenty-five years. Her books include *Savoring the Seasons of the Northern Heartland* (coauthored with Lucia Watson), *The Northern Heartland Kitchen,* and *Minnesota's Bounty: The Farmers Market Cookbook,* all published by the University of Minnesota Press.

Mette Nielsen is a food and farm photographer who has covered both regional and national assignments for more than thirty years. Her photography has been featured in several books, including *Minnesota's Bounty: The Farmers Market Cookbook* and *The Spoonriver Cookbook,* both published by the University of Minnesota Press.

Notes

Notes

Notes

Notes